contents

prawn, snow pea and wild rice salad

PREPARATION TIME 20 MINUTES **COOKING TIME** 20 MINUTES

24 uncooked medium king prawns (1kg)
1½ cups (300g) white and wild rice blend
150g snow peas, trimmed, halved lengthways
1 small red onion (100g), sliced thinly
½ cup coarsely chopped fresh flat-leaf parsley
150g snow pea tendrils

RASPBERRY VINEGAR DRESSING
⅓ cup (80ml) raspberry vinegar
2 tablespoons olive oil
1 tablespoon dijon mustard
2 cloves garlic, crushed
2 tablespoons lemon juice
2 teaspoons sugar

1 Shell and devein prawns, leaving tails intact.
2 Make raspberry vinegar dressing.
3 Cook rice in large saucepan of boiling water, uncovered, until tender; drain.
4 Meanwhile, boil, steam or microwave peas until just tender.
5 Cook prawns on heated lightly oiled grill plate (or grill or barbecue) until changed in colour.
6 Place rice, peas and prawns in large bowl with onion, parsley, tendrils and dressing; toss gently to combine.
   RASPBERRY VINEGAR DRESSING Place ingredients in screw-top jar; shake well.

serves 4
per serving 10.5g fat; 2096kJ (500 cal)

THE AUSTRALIAN Women's Weekly

Simple, fresh and light... it has certainly become the fashion now, where we allow the natural flavours of ingredients to dominate without covering them with heavy creams and sauces. Another wonderful thing about light food is that it's quick and easy to prepare – as you can tell by looking through the pages of this book, simplicity can be beautiful on its own when you're using the best ingredients. So, next time your family wants something light and refreshing for dinner, turn to *Lean Food* for its fresh, tasty and low-fat recipes.

Pamela Clark

Food Director

grilled tuna with soba

PREPARATION TIME 15 MINUTES **COOKING TIME** 10 MINUTES

Soba are Japanese
buckwheat noodles similar
in appearance to spaghetti.
They are available dried
from Asian food stores
and some supermarkets.

4 x 200g tuna steaks
½ cup (125ml) mirin
2 teaspoons wasabi paste
½ cup (125ml) japanese soy sauce
1 sheet toasted seaweed (yaki-nori)
300g soba
6 green onions, sliced thinly
2 fresh long red chillies, chopped finely

1 Combine tuna with 2 tablespoons of the mirin, half of the wasabi and half of the soy sauce in large bowl; toss to coat tuna in marinade. Cover; refrigerate 10 minutes.

2 Meanwhile, using scissors, cut seaweed into four strips; cut each strip crossways into thin pieces.

3 Cook soba in large saucepan of boiling water, uncovered, until just tender; drain. Rinse under cold water; drain.

4 Meanwhile, cook tuna on heated lightly oiled grill plate (or grill or barbecue) until browned both sides and cooked as desired.

5 Combine soba in medium bowl with onion, chilli and combined remaining mirin, wasabi and sauce. Serve soba with tuna and seaweed.

serves 4
per serving 12.3g fat; 2423kJ (579 cal)

roasted tomato and capsicum soup with tortilla strips

PREPARATION TIME 20 MINUTES **COOKING TIME** 35 MINUTES

2 large red capsicums (700g)

5 large vine-ripened tomatoes (1.2kg), halved

1 tablespoon olive oil

1 medium brown onion (150g), chopped coarsely

2 cloves garlic, crushed

4 fresh long red chillies, chopped coarsely

2 cups (500ml) water

2 cups (500ml) prepared vegetable stock

2 corn tortillas, cut into 1cm strips

cooking-oil spray

2 tablespoons light sour cream

2 tablespoons finely chopped fresh chives

1 Preheat oven to very hot.

2 Quarter capsicums, discard seeds and membranes. Roast capsicum, skin-side up, and tomato, cut-side up, on lightly oiled oven trays, uncovered, in very hot oven about 15 minutes or until capsicum skin blisters and blackens and tomato softens. Cover capsicum pieces with plastic or paper for 5 minutes; peel away skin, cover to keep warm. Cool tomato 5 minutes; peel away skin.

3 Heat oil in large saucepan; cook onion, garlic and chilli, stirring, until onion softens. Add capsicum and tomato; cook, stirring, 5 minutes. Add the water and stock; bring to a boil. Reduce heat; simmer, uncovered, 10 minutes.

4 Meanwhile, place tortilla strips, in single layer, on lightly oiled oven tray. Spray with cooking-oil spray; grill until browned lightly and crisp.

5 Blend or process tomato mixture, in batches, until smooth, then pass through food mill (mouli) or fine sieve into large saucepan; discard solids.

6 Divide soup among serving bowls; top with sour cream and chives. Serve with tortilla strips.

serves 4
per serving 8.5g fat; 664kJ (159 cal)

TIP Warm any remaining corn tortillas in your microwave oven and serve them with the soup.

marinated lamb backstraps
with lentil and rocket salad

PREPARATION TIME 15 MINUTES (PLUS REFRIGERATION TIME) **COOKING TIME** 15 MINUTES

Puy lentils are from the region of the same name in France. Very small and particularly fast cooking, they have a delicate, almost nut-like flavour.

4 x 200g lamb backstraps, trimmed
⅓ cup (80ml) balsamic vinegar
4 cloves garlic, crushed
¼ cup finely chopped fresh thyme
1 cup (200g) puy lentils
6 large egg tomatoes (540g), chopped finely
100g baby rocket leaves
1 tablespoon finely grated lemon rind
2 tablespoons lemon juice

1 Combine lamb, vinegar, garlic and half of the thyme in large bowl; toss to coat lamb in marinade. Cover; refrigerate 3 hours or overnight.
2 Cook lentils in medium saucepan of boiling water, uncovered, until tender; drain.
3 Meanwhile, cook drained lamb on heated lightly oiled grill plate (or grill or barbecue) until browned both sides and cooked as desired. Cover lamb; stand 5 minutes then slice thickly.
4 Place lentils in large bowl with tomato, rocket, rind, juice and remaining thyme; toss gently to combine. Divide salad among serving plates; top with lamb.

serves 4
per serving 8.6g fat; 1692kJ (404 cal)

butterflied pork steaks with pear and apple salsa

PREPARATION TIME 15 MINUTES **COOKING TIME** 10 MINUTES

1 tablespoon water
2 tablespoons lemon juice
2 teaspoons sugar
1 medium green apple (150g),
    diced into 1cm pieces
1 medium red apple (150g),
    diced into 1cm pieces
1 small pear (180g), peeled,
    diced into 1cm pieces
1 long green chilli, seeded,
    chopped finely
1 tablespoon finely chopped
    fresh mint
8 x 100g butterflied pork
    steaks, trimmed

1 Combine the water, juice and
   sugar in medium bowl, stirring,
   until sugar dissolves. Add apples,
   pear, chilli and mint; toss gently
   to combine.
2 Cook pork on heated lightly oiled
   grill plate (or grill or barbecue)
   until browned both sides and
   cooked as desired. Serve pork
   with salsa.

serves 4
per serving 7.9g fat;
1268kJ (303 cal)

mushroom and asparagus salad

PREPARATION TIME 15 MINUTES **COOKING TIME** 20 MINUTES

Swiss brown mushrooms, also known as cremini or roman mushrooms, are similar in appearance to button mushrooms, but are a slightly dark brown in colour. The large variety are often known as portobello mushrooms.

400g swiss brown mushrooms
200g fresh shiitake mushrooms
500g green asparagus, trimmed
500g white asparagus, trimmed
2 teaspoons finely grated
    lemon rind
¼ cup (60ml) lemon juice
2 tablespoons olive oil
1 clove garlic, crushed
1 cup loosely packed fresh
    flat-leaf parsley leaves
2 tablespoons toasted
    pine nuts

1 Cook mushrooms and asparagus, in batches, on heated lightly oiled grill plate (or grill or barbecue) until browned and just tender.
2 Meanwhile, place rind, juice, oil and garlic in screw-top jar; shake well.
3 Combine vegetables in large bowl with parsley, nuts and dressing; toss gently to combine.

serves 4
per serving 14.8g fat;
908kJ (217 cal)

barramundi with kipflers and roasted capsicum

PREPARATION TIME 25 MINUTES **COOKING TIME** 40 MINUTES

We used a whole barramundi for this recipe, but any whole, firm, white-fleshed large fish can be used.

½ cup (125ml) prepared vegetable stock
1 tablespoon lemon juice
700g kipfler potatoes, halved lengthways
1 tablespoon finely grated lemon rind
⅓ cup coarsely chopped fresh oregano
1.2kg whole barramundi, cleaned
1 large red capsicum (350g), sliced thinly
1 large yellow capsicum (350g), sliced thinly
2 cloves garlic, crushed

1 Preheat oven to moderate.
2 Combine stock, juice and potato in large baking dish; roast, uncovered, in moderate oven 10 minutes.
3 Meanwhile, combine rind and oregano in small bowl. Score fish both sides; press rind mixture into cuts and inside cavity.
4 Place fish in lightly oiled large baking dish; roast, uncovered, in moderate oven about 30 minutes.
5 Meanwhile, add capsicums and garlic to potato mixture; stir to combine. Roast, uncovered, in moderate oven about 30 minutes or until potato is tender. Serve fish with vegetables, drizzled with any pan juices; sprinkle fish with oregano leaves, if desired.

serves 4
per serving 2.4g fat; 1279kJ (306 cal)

lemon thyme chicken with spinach and pea pilaf

PREPARATION TIME 10 MINUTES **COOKING TIME** 50 MINUTES

4 x 170g single chicken breast fillets
1 tablespoon coarsely chopped fresh thyme
2 teaspoons finely grated lemon rind
1 tablespoon lemon juice
1 tablespoon olive oil
1 large brown onion (200g), sliced thinly
1 clove garlic, crushed
1½ cups (300g) long-grain brown rice
2½ cups (625ml) water
3 cups (750ml) prepared chicken stock
150g baby spinach leaves
1 cup (125g) frozen peas, thawed
2 teaspoons coarsely chopped fresh thyme, extra
1 tablespoon finely grated lemon rind, extra

1 Combine chicken, thyme, rind, juice and half of the oil in medium bowl; toss to coat chicken in marinade. Cover; refrigerate 10 minutes.
2 Meanwhile, heat remaining oil in large deep non-stick frying pan; cook onion and garlic, stirring, until onion softens. Add rice; cook, stirring, 1 minute. Add the water and stock; bring to a boil. Reduce heat; simmer, covered, about 45 minutes or until liquid is absorbed and rice is cooked as desired.
3 Meanwhile, cook chicken on heated lightly oiled grill plate (or grill or barbecue) until browned both sides and cooked through. Cover; stand 5 minutes then slice thickly.
4 Stir spinach, peas, extra thyme and extra rind into pilaf. Divide pilaf among serving plates; top with chicken.

serves 4
per serving 11.3g fat; 2353kJ (562 cal)

pasta salad with roasted vegetables in chilli cream sauce

PREPARATION TIME 25 MINUTES **COOKING TIME** 30 MINUTES

Pappardelle is a long, flat, fairly wide pasta sometimes scalloped along its long sides. It can be used layered like lasagne or, as here, tossed with vegetables and a rich creamy sauce.

2 medium red capsicums (400g)
2 medium yellow capsicums (400g)
375g pappardelle
6 baby eggplants (360g), sliced thickly
2 flat mushrooms (160g)
180g haloumi, sliced thinly
1 cup loosely packed fresh basil leaves

CHILLI CREAM SAUCE
10 large egg tomatoes (900g), halved
2 cloves garlic, crushed
4 fresh small red thai chillies, sliced thinly
2 tablespoons cream

1 Preheat oven to very hot. Make chilli cream sauce.
2 Meanwhile, quarter capsicums; discard seeds and membranes. Roast under grill or in very hot oven, skin-side up, until skin blisters and blackens. Cover capsicum pieces with plastic or paper for 5 minutes; peel away skin then slice capsicum thickly.
3 Cook pasta in large saucepan of boiling water, uncovered, until tender.
4 Meanwhile, cook eggplant, mushrooms and cheese, in batches, on heated lightly oiled grill plate (or grill or barbecue) until browned and just tender. Slice mushrooms thickly; chop cheese coarsely.
5 Combine vegetables, cheese and drained pasta in large bowl with basil; stir in sauce. Sprinkle with fresh basil leaves, if desired.
CHILLI CREAM SAUCE Line two oven trays with baking paper. Place tomato, cut-side up, in single layer, on prepared trays; roast, uncovered, in very hot oven about 20 minutes or until softened. Blend or process half of the tomato with garlic, chilli and cream until pureed. Chop remaining tomato coarsely; stir into sauce.

serves 4
per serving 13.8g fat; 2385kJ (570 cal)

char-grilled scallops with citrus salsa

PREPARATION TIME 15 MINUTES **COOKING TIME** 10 MINUTES

32 scallops (800g), roe removed
1 small pink grapefruit (350g),
    chopped finely
1 large orange (300g),
    chopped finely
1 lime, chopped finely
1 small mango (300g),
    chopped finely
¼ cup finely chopped
    fresh thai basil
¼ cup finely chopped
    fresh mint

CITRUS DRESSING
2 tablespoons mirin
1 tablespoon orange juice
1 tablespoon lemon juice
1 tablespoon olive oil
1 teaspoon finely grated
    lime rind

1 Cook scallops, in batches,
  on heated lightly oiled grill
  plate (or grill or barbecue)
  until browned both sides and
  cooked as desired.
2 Meanwhile, make citrus dressing.
3 Place remaining ingredients in
  medium bowl with half of the
  dressing; toss gently to combine.
4 Serve scallops with salsa; drizzle
  with remaining dressing.
  CITRUS DRESSING Place
  ingredients in screw-top jar;
  shake well.

serves 4
per serving 5.7g fat;
756kJ (181 cal)

spice-rubbed beef fillet with chickpea and preserved lemon salad

PREPARATION TIME 20 MINUTES (PLUS REFRIGERATION TIME) **COOKING TIME** 15 MINUTES

Kalonji, also known as nigella, are black, teardrop-shaped seeds used extensively in Indian cooking to impart a sharp, almost nutty flavour.

1 teaspoon coriander seeds
1 teaspoon kalonji seeds
1 teaspoon dried chilli flakes
1 teaspoon sea salt
1 clove garlic, crushed
600g piece beef eye
    fillet, trimmed
6 large egg tomatoes
    (540g), peeled
425g can chickpeas,
    rinsed, drained
2 tablespoons finely chopped
    preserved lemon rind
⅔ cup loosely packed fresh
    flat-leaf parsley leaves
⅔ cup loosely packed fresh
    coriander leaves
1 tablespoon lemon juice

1 Using mortar and pestle, crush seeds, chilli, salt and garlic into coarse paste; rub paste into beef. Cover; refrigerate 20 minutes.
2 Meanwhile, quarter tomatoes; discard seeds and pulp. Chop tomato flesh finely. Combine in medium bowl with chickpeas, rind, herbs and juice.
3 Cook beef on lightly oiled heated grill plate (or grill or barbecue) until browned all over and cooked as desired. Cover; stand 10 minutes then slice thinly. Serve beef on salad.

serves 4
per serving 8g fat;
1166kJ (279 cal)

mexican chicken with black bean and barley salad

PREPARATION TIME 10 MINUTES **COOKING TIME** 45 MINUTES

Black beans, also known as turtle beans, are Cuban or Latin American rather than Chinese in origin. Jet black with a tiny white eye, black beans can be found, either packaged or loose, in most greengrocers and delicatessens.

½ cup (100g) dried black beans
2 cups (500ml) prepared chicken stock
1 litre (4 cups) water
¾ cup (165g) pearl barley
35g packet taco seasoning mix
⅓ cup (80ml) prepared chicken stock, extra
4 x 170g single chicken breast fillets
1 large red capsicum (350g), chopped finely
1 clove garlic, crushed
¼ cup (60ml) lime juice
2 teaspoons olive oil
½ cup loosely packed fresh coriander leaves

1 Preheat oven to moderately hot.
2 Combine beans with half of the stock and half of the water in medium saucepan; bring to a boil. Reduce heat; simmer, uncovered, about 45 minutes or until tender, drain. Rinse under cold water; drain.
3 Meanwhile, combine barley with remaining stock and remaining water in medium saucepan; bring to a boil. Reduce heat; simmer, uncovered, until just tender; drain. Rinse under cold water; drain.
4 Blend seasoning with extra stock in medium bowl, add chicken; toss to coat chicken in mixture. Drain chicken; reserve marinade. Place chicken, in single layer, on metal rack in large shallow baking dish; bake, uncovered, in moderately hot oven about 30 minutes or until cooked through, brushing with reserved marinade halfway through cooking time. Cover; stand 5 minutes then slice thickly.
5 Place beans and barley in large bowl with remaining ingredients; toss gently to combine. Divide salad among serving plates; top with chicken.

serves 4
per serving 8.5g fat; 1826kJ (436 cal)

roast veal rack with herb stuffing

PREPARATION TIME 20 MINUTES **COOKING TIME** 35 MINUTES

1 small brown onion (80g), chopped finely

1 clove garlic, crushed

½ trimmed celery stalk (50g), chopped finely

¾ cup (45g) stale breadcrumbs

1 tablespoon dijon mustard

1 teaspoon finely chopped fresh thyme

1 tablespoon finely chopped fresh flat-leaf parsley

1 teaspoon finely grated lemon rind

2 teaspoons sea salt

2 teaspoons cracked black pepper

800g veal rack (4 cutlets), trimmed

1 medium brown onion (150g), chopped coarsely

1½ cups (375ml) prepared beef stock

2 teaspoons olive oil

2 teaspoons balsamic vinegar

½ cup (125ml) prepared beef stock, extra

1 Preheat oven to hot.

2 Cook finely chopped onion, garlic and celery in heated lightly oiled small non-stick frying pan, stirring, until vegetables soften. Add breadcrumbs; cook until breadcrumbs brown lightly. Remove from heat; stir in mustard, herbs, rind, half of the salt and half of the pepper. Cool 10 minutes.

3 Using sharp knife, make a tunnel through veal rack, close to the bone; fill with herb mixture.

4 Place coarsely chopped onion and stock in large flameproof baking dish; add veal, drizzle with oil, sprinkle with remaining salt and pepper. Roast, uncovered, in hot oven about 30 minutes or until cooked as desired. Remove veal from dish, cover; stand 10 minutes.

5 Stir vinegar and extra stock into veal juices in dish; bring to a boil. Strain into medium jug; serve with veal and steamed green beans, if desired.

serves 4

per serving 7.9g fat; 1158kJ (277 cal)

stuffed capsicums with lentils

PREPARATION TIME 15 MINUTES **COOKING TIME** 30 MINUTES

1 tablespoon olive oil
1 small brown onion (80g), chopped finely
1 clove garlic, crushed
1 small carrot (70g), chopped finely
1 small green zucchini (90g), chopped finely
¼ cup (60ml) water
¼ cup (50g) red lentils
¼ cup (55g) risoni
1 tablespoon tomato paste
1 cup (250ml) prepared vegetable stock
12 baby red capsicums (540g)
2 tablespoons finely grated parmesan cheese

1 Preheat oven to hot.
2 Heat oil in large saucepan; cook onion and garlic, stirring, until onion softens. Add carrot and zucchini; cook, stirring, until vegetables are tender. Stir in the water, lentils, risoni, paste and stock; bring to a boil. Reduce heat; simmer, uncovered, about 10 minutes or until lentils are tender.
3 Meanwhile, carefully cut tops off capsicums; discard tops. Discard seeds and membranes, leaving capsicums intact; roast, uncovered, on baking-paper-lined oven tray in hot oven about 15 minutes or until just softened.
4 Divide lentil mixture among capsicums; sprinkle with cheese. Place under preheated grill until cheese melts.

serves 4
per serving 6.6g fat; 771kJ (184 cal)

seafood skewers with radicchio and fennel salad

PREPARATION TIME 25 MINUTES (PLUS REFRIGERATION TIME) **COOKING TIME** 10 MINUTES

You need to soak eight bamboo skewers in water for at least an hour before use to prevent splintering and scorching. Any firm white fish fillet, such as ling or blue-eye, can be used in this recipe.

8 uncooked large king prawns (560g)
8 cleaned baby octopus (720g)
400g firm white fish fillets
8 scallops (200g), roe removed
2 teaspoons fennel seeds
2 teaspoons dried green peppercorns
2 tablespoons white wine vinegar
2 cloves garlic, crushed
1 tablespoon olive oil
2 medium radicchio (400g)
2 small fennel (400g), trimmed, sliced thinly
1 cup firmly packed fresh flat-leaf parsley leaves

MUSTARD DRESSING
¼ cup (60ml) white wine vinegar
½ teaspoon mustard powder
1 tablespoon olive oil
1 teaspoon sugar
4 green onions, chopped coarsely

1 Shell and devein prawns, leaving tails intact. Remove heads and beaks from octopus. Cut fish into 2.5cm pieces. Combine seafood in large bowl.
2 Using mortar and pestle, crush seeds and peppercorns coarsely, add to seafood with vinegar, garlic and oil; toss gently to combine. Cover; refrigerate 3 hours or overnight.
3 Make mustard dressing.
4 Thread seafood, alternating varieties, on skewers; cook on heated lightly oiled grill plate (or grill or barbecue) until seafood is just changed in colour and cooked as desired.
5 Meanwhile, discard dark outer leaves of radicchio, tear inner leaves roughly. Combine radicchio in medium bowl with fennel, parsley and dressing; toss gently to combine. Serve seafood skewers on salad.
MUSTARD DRESSING Place ingredients in screw-top jar; shake well.

serves 4
per serving 14g fat; 1877kJ (448 cal)

TIP Use green peppercorns in brine if you can't find the dried variety; rinse then drain them thoroughly before using.

chicken with bok choy and flat mushrooms

PREPARATION TIME 10 MINUTES **COOKING TIME** 25 MINUTES

2 tablespoons honey

⅓ cup (80ml) soy sauce

2 tablespoons dry sherry

1 teaspoon five-spice powder

4cm piece fresh ginger (20g), grated

1 tablespoon peanut oil

4 x 170g single chicken breast fillets

4 flat mushrooms (360g)

500g baby bok choy, quartered lengthways

1 cup (250ml) prepared chicken stock

2 teaspoons cornflour

2 tablespoons water

1 Combine honey, soy sauce, sherry, five-spice, ginger and oil in small jug. Place chicken in medium bowl with half of the honey mixture; toss to coat chicken in marinade. Cover; refrigerate 10 minutes.

2 Meanwhile, cook mushrooms and bok choy, in batches, on heated lightly oiled grill plate (or grill or barbecue) until just tender; cover to keep warm.

3 Cook drained chicken on same lightly oiled grill plate (or grill or barbecue) until browned both sides and cooked through. Cover; stand 5 minutes then slice thickly.

4 Meanwhile, combine remaining honey mixture in small saucepan with stock; bring to a boil. Stir in blended cornflour and water; cook, stirring, until sauce boils and thickens slightly.

5 Divide mushrooms and bok choy among serving plates; top with chicken, drizzle with sauce. Serve with steamed rice, if desired.

serves 4

per serving 9.3g fat; 1424kJ (340 cal)

sumac and sesame-grilled blue-eye with fattoush

PREPARATION TIME 30 MINUTES **COOKING TIME** 10 MINUTES

Sumac is used extensively in kitchens from the eastern Mediterranean through to Pakistan. Both in cooking and as a condiment, sumac's tart astringency adds a delightful piquancy to food without the heat of a chilli. We used blue-eye cutlets, but any firm white fish can be used for this recipe.

1 tablespoon sesame seeds
2 teaspoons dried chilli flakes
1 tablespoon sumac
2 teaspoons sea salt flakes
4 x 200g blue-eye cutlets
1 lemon, cut into wedges

FATTOUSH
6 pocket pitta
4 small tomatoes (520g), chopped coarsely
1 large green capsicum (350g), chopped coarsely
2 lebanese cucumbers (260g), seeded, chopped coarsely
4 red radishes (140g), sliced thinly
4 green onions, sliced thinly
1½ cups firmly packed fresh flat-leaf parsley leaves
½ cup coarsely chopped fresh mint
1 tablespoon olive oil
¼ cup (60ml) lemon juice
2 cloves garlic, crushed

1 Make fattoush.
2 Meanwhile, combine seeds, chilli, sumac, salt and fish in large bowl; toss to coat fish in spice mixture. Cook fish on heated oiled grill plate (or grill or barbecue) until cooked as desired. Serve fish with lemon and fattoush.
   FATTOUSH Preheat oven to moderately hot. Split pitta in half horizontally; cut halves into 2.5cm pieces. Place pitta on oven tray; toast, uncovered, in moderately hot oven until browned lightly. Combine pitta in large bowl with tomato, capsicum, cucumber, radish, onion and herbs. Place oil, juice and garlic in screw-top jar; shake well. Add dressing to fattoush; toss gently to combine.

serves 4
per serving 13.9g fat; 2733kJ (653 cal)

raw

japanese-style tuna with red-maple radish

PREPARATION TIME 25 MINUTES

Tuna sold as sashimi has to meet stringent guidelines regarding its handling and treatment after leaving the water. Nevertheless, it is best to seek local advice from authorities before eating any raw seafood. The combination of daikon and chilli treated in this way is commonly known in Japan as "red-maple radish". It can be used as an accompaniment to any Japanese dish using raw fish.

600g piece sashimi tuna
⅓ cup (80ml) rice vinegar
½ small daikon (200g)
4 dried long red chillies, chopped finely
2 tablespoons mirin
1 teaspoon sesame oil
1 teaspoon black sesame seeds
1 sheet toasted seaweed (yaki-nori), shredded finely

1 Slice tuna as thinly as possible; place, in single layer, on large platter, drizzle with vinegar. Cover; refrigerate until required.
2 Meanwhile, grate peeled daikon finely. Place daikon and chilli in fine sieve set over small bowl; stir with small wooden spoon to combine then press with back of spoon to extract as much daikon liquid as possible.
3 Drain vinegar from tuna. Divide tuna among serving plates; drizzle with combined mirin and oil; sprinkle with seeds. Serve tuna with red-maple radish and seaweed.

serves 4
per serving 10.3g fat; 1171kJ (280 cal)

crudités with four dips

PREPARATION TIME 50 MINUTES

1 medium red capsicum (200g)
1 medium yellow capsicum (200g)
4 trimmed celery stalks (400g)
200g snow peas, trimmed
2 lebanese cucumbers (260g)
15 baby carrots (300g), peeled

1 Remove seeds and membranes from capsicums. Chop a quarter of the red capsicum finely; reserve for cornichon dip. Slice remaining red capsicum and yellow capsicum into thick strips. Halve celery stalks; cut into thin strips. Halve cucumbers lengthways; discard seeds, cut into thick strips.

2 Divide vegetables among serving platter; serve with dips.

cornichon dip

Combine 2 tablespoons finely chopped drained cornichons, 2 finely chopped green onions, 1 tablespoon finely chopped drained capers, ¾ cup low-fat cottage cheese and 2 teaspoons dijon mustard in small bowl with reserved red capsicum.

makes 1 cup
per tablespoon 0.2g fat; 65kJ (16 cal)

ricotta and green olive dip

Combine ½ cup low-fat ricotta, ¼ cup finely chopped seeded green olives, 1 crushed clove garlic, ¼ cup finely chopped fresh chives, ¼ cup finely chopped fresh flat-leaf parsley, 1 teaspoon finely grated lemon rind and 1 tablespoon lemon juice in small bowl.

makes 1 cup
per tablespoon 1g fat; 75kJ (18 cal)

tzatziki

Combine 2 seeded coarsely grated drained lebanese cucumbers, ¾ cup yogurt and 1 crushed clove garlic in small bowl.

makes 1 cup
per tablespoon   0.6g fat; 60kJ (14 cal)

beetroot dip

Combine 2 finely grated medium beetroots, ⅓ cup light sour cream and 1 teaspoon red wine vinegar in small bowl.

makes 1 cup
per tablespoon   1.3g fat; 102kJ (24 cal)

vegetable and cottage cheese terrine

PREPARATION TIME 40 MINUTES (PLUS REFRIGERATION TIME)

Buy zucchini just large enough to make 13cm-long strips once trimmed and sliced.

2½ cups (500g) cottage cheese
1 small yellow zucchini (90g),
  grated coarsely
4 green onions, chopped finely
1 tablespoon finely shredded
  fresh basil
1 tablespoon finely chopped
  fresh oregano
1 teaspoon finely chopped
  fresh thyme
1 clove garlic, crushed
1 teaspoon lemon juice
1 large green zucchini (150g)
1 large yellow zucchini (150g)
20g baby spinach leaves,
  shredded coarsely
2 teaspoons olive oil

CAPSICUM AND
TOMATO SAUCE
2 medium tomatoes (380g),
  chopped finely
1 small yellow capsicum (150g),
  chopped finely
2 green onions, chopped finely
1 tablespoon finely shredded
  fresh basil
1 clove garlic, crushed
2 teaspoons olive oil
2 teaspoons lemon juice

1 Drain cheese in muslin-lined strainer or colander set over large bowl. Cover then weight cheese with an upright saucer topped with a heavy can. Drain overnight in refrigerator; discard liquid.

2 Line base and two long sides of 8cm x 25cm bar pan with baking paper or plastic wrap, extending paper 5cm above sides of pan.

3 Combine drained cheese in medium bowl with grated zucchini, onion, herbs, garlic and juice.

4 Discard ends of both large zucchini; using vegetable peeler, slice into thin strips (discard outer strips of both zucchini).

5 Overlap alternate-coloured zucchini strips in prepared pan, starting from centre of base and extending over both long sides. Cover both short sides of pan with alternate-coloured zucchini strips, ensuring slices overlap to cover corners and extend over both short sides.

6 Spread half of the cheese mixture into zucchini-lined pan; cover with spinach, carefully spread remaining cheese mixture over spinach. Fold zucchini strips at short sides over filling then repeat with strips over long sides to completely enclose filling (mixture will be slightly higher than pan). Cover terrine tightly with foil; refrigerate 1 hour.

7 Meanwhile, make capsicum and tomato sauce.

8 Turn terrine onto serving plate; drizzle with oil. Using fine serrated knife, cut terrine crossways into thick slices; serve with sauce.
CAPSICUM AND TOMATO SAUCE Combine ingredients in small bowl.

serves 4
per serving 12.3g fat; 971kJ (232 cal)

TIP Do not add any salt to the cottage-cheese mixture as this will cause the filling to become too wet.
SERVING SUGGESTION Serve with a salad of baby rocket and baby spinach leaves, if desired.

sashimi stacks

PREPARATION TIME 30 MINUTES

Use the freshest, sashimi-quality fish you can find. Salmon sold as sashimi has to meet stringent guidelines regarding its handling and treatment after leaving the water. We suggest you seek local advice from authorities before eating any raw seafood.

½ lebanese cucumber
(65g), seeded
½ medium avocado (125g)
400g piece sashimi salmon
1 teaspoon wasabi paste
4 green onions, quartered
lengthways
½ sheet toasted seaweed
(yaki-nori), cut into 1cm strips
2 teaspoons toasted
sesame seeds
2 tablespoons japanese
soy sauce

1 Cut cucumber and avocado into long thin strips.
2 Cut salmon into 32 thin slices.
3 Place 16 slices of the salmon on serving platter; spread each with a little wasabi then divide cucumber, avocado and onion among slices. Top each stack with one remaining salmon slice.
4 Wrap seaweed strip around each stack; sprinkle each with sesame seeds. Serve sashimi stacks with soy sauce.

makes 16
per serving 3.2g fat;
214kJ (51 cal)

TIP Use scissors to cut the seaweed into strips.

mixed sashimi

PREPARATION TIME 45 MINUTES

As seen at left, exercise caution before eating any raw seafood. Daikon is a type of radish with a sweet, fresh flavour. Its white flesh is crisp and juicy, while its skin can be either creamy white or black. Refrigerate, in a plastic bag, up to a week.

½ small daikon (200g)
300g piece sashimi tuna
300g piece sashimi salmon
300g piece sashimi kingfish
1 teaspoon wasabi paste
2 tablespoons japanese pink
  pickled ginger
⅓ cup (80ml) japanese
  soy sauce

1 Shred daikon finely; place in bowl of iced water. Reserve.

2 Place tuna on chopping board; using sharp knife, cut 6mm slices at right angles to the grain of the tuna, holding the piece of tuna with your fingers and slicing with the knife almost vertical to the board. Repeat with salmon and kingfish.

3 Divide drained daikon and fish among serving plates; serve with wasabi, ginger and soy sauce.

serves 4
per serving 11.5g fat;
1418kJ (339 cal)

oysters with toppings

Each of the toppings makes enough for 24 oysters served on the half shell. We used rock oysters for this recipe; if you use smaller oysters, there may be leftover topping. All recipes take about 10 minutes to prepare.

chilli-lime dressing

Place ½ teaspoon finely grated lime rind, ¼ cup lime juice, 2 teaspoons sugar, 1 finely shredded kaffir lime leaf, 2 small thinly sliced fresh red thai chillies and 2 tablespoons peanut oil in screw-top jar; shake well. Top oysters with dressing.

per oyster 1.8g fat; 94kJ (23 cal)

tomato-capsicum salsa

Combine 2 small finely chopped seeded vine-ripened tomatoes, 1 small finely chopped red onion, 1 small finely chopped green capsicum, ¼ cup tomato juice, ¼ cup lemon juice, 1 teaspoon Tabasco, 1 tablespoon olive oil and 2 crushed cloves garlic in small bowl. Top oysters with salsa.

per oyster 1g fat; 77kJ (18 cal)

green olive paste

Blend or process ½ cup seeded green olives,
2 teaspoons olive oil, ¼ cup red wine vinegar,
2 quartered cloves garlic and 2 tablespoons
toasted pine nuts until mixture forms a paste.
Top oysters with paste; sprinkle with 2 teaspoons
coarsely chopped fresh lemon thyme.

per oyster 1.5g fat; 94kJ (23 cal)

lemon-garlic dressing

Place 2 teaspoons finely grated lemon rind,
¼ cup lemon juice, 2 crushed cloves garlic,
1 tablespoon olive oil and 1 tablespoon finely
chopped fresh chives in screw-top jar; shake well.
Top oysters with dressing.

per oyster 1g fat; 63kJ (15 cal)

pear, walnut and fetta salad with walnut oil dressing

PREPARATION TIME 20 MINUTES

3 medium pears (700g)
2 tablespoons coarsely
    chopped toasted walnuts
1 butter lettuce, trimmed, torn
½ cup (25g) snow pea sprouts
100g fetta cheese, crumbled

WALNUT OIL DRESSING
1 tablespoon walnut oil
2 teaspoons wholegrain
    mustard
2 tablespoons white
    wine vinegar
1 clove garlic, crushed
1 tablespoon finely
    chopped fresh chives

1   Make walnut oil dressing.
2   Core pears; slice pears into thin
    wedges. Place in large bowl
    with remaining ingredients and
    dressing; toss gently to combine.
WALNUT OIL DRESSING
Place ingredients in screw-top
jar; shake well.

serves 4
per serving 13.9g fat;
968kJ (231 cal)

TIP We used beurre bosc pears
in our recipe, but you can use
any variety you prefer.

gazpacho

PREPARATION TIME 25 MINUTES (PLUS REFRIGERATION TIME)

A chilled soup originating in the southern province of Andalusia in Spain, gazpacho has a wonderfully refreshing flavour.

3 cups (750ml) tomato juice
8 medium egg tomatoes (600g),
    chopped coarsely
1 medium red onion (170g),
    chopped coarsely
1 clove garlic, quartered
1 lebanese cucumber (130g),
    chopped coarsely
1 small red capsicum (150g),
    chopped coarsely
2 teaspoons Tabasco
4 green onions, chopped finely
½ lebanese cucumber (65g),
    seeded, chopped finely
½ small yellow capsicum (75g),
    chopped finely
2 teaspoons olive oil
1 tablespoon vodka
2 tablespoons finely chopped
    fresh coriander

1 Blend or process juice, tomato, onion, garlic, coarsely chopped cucumber and red capsicum, in batches, until pureed. Strain through sieve into large bowl, cover; refrigerate soup 3 hours.
2 Combine remaining ingredients in small bowl. Divide soup among serving bowls; top with vegetable mixture.

serves 4
per serving 2.7g fat;
511kJ (122 cal)

TIP Gazpacho can be made a day ahead and kept covered in the refrigerator.

cabbage, fennel and carrot salad with orange-herb dressing

PREPARATION TIME 20 MINUTES

You need to buy a quarter of a medium red cabbage and a medium chinese cabbage for this recipe.

4 trimmed celery stalks (400g)
2 medium carrots (240g)
2 small fennel (400g), trimmed, sliced thinly
4 trimmed red radishes (60g), sliced thinly
1½ cups (120g) finely shredded red cabbage
5 cups (400g) coarsely shredded chinese cabbage
1 cup loosely packed fresh basil leaves
1 cup loosely packed fresh mint leaves
¼ cup (40g) pepitas

ORANGE-HERB DRESSING
1 tablespoon finely chopped fresh flat-leaf parsley
4 green onions, chopped coarsely
½ teaspoon finely grated orange rind
⅓ cup (80ml) orange juice
2 tablespoons raspberry vinegar
2 cloves garlic, crushed
1 tablespoon peanut oil

1 Make orange-herb dressing.
2 Cut celery and carrot into 6cm lengths; using vegetable peeler, slice celery and carrot into ribbons.
3 Place ribbons in large bowl with fennel, radish, cabbages, herbs and dressing; toss gently to combine. Sprinkle with pepitas.
ORANGE-HERB DRESSING Place ingredients in screw-top jar; shake well.

serves 4
per serving 10.2g fat; 731kJ (175 cal)

juices and frappés

Preparation time for each of these juices and frappés is about 20 minutes; each serves 4 and makes 2 litres.

orange, apple and ginger juice

6 medium oranges (1.5kg), peeled,
   chopped coarsely
5 large apples (1kg), cored, chopped coarsely
4 large carrots (720g), chopped coarsely
10cm piece fresh ginger (50g), peeled

Push ingredients through juice extractor.
Stir to combine.

per serving 0.7g fat; 978kJ (234 cal)

beetroot, carrot and spinach juice

6 medium beetroots (1kg), peeled,
   chopped coarsely
5 large carrots (1kg), chopped coarsely
600g spinach, trimmed, chopped coarsely

Push ingredients through juice extractor.
Stir to combine.

per serving 0.7g fat; 661kJ (158 cal)

kiwi fruit, orange and mint frappé

You need a medium pineapple for this recipe.

600g coarsely chopped pineapple pieces
6 kiwi fruit (500g), halved
1 cup loosely packed fresh mint leaves
2 cups (500ml) orange juice
4 cups crushed ice
¼ cup finely shredded fresh mint

Blend or process pineapple, kiwi fruit, mint leaves,
juice and ice, in batches, until almost smooth.
Combine batches in large jug. Top glasses with
shredded mint.

per serving 0.7g fat; 658kJ (157 cal)

watermelon and pineapple frappé

You need half a small seedless watermelon
for this recipe.

650g coarsely chopped seedless
   watermelon pieces
2½ cups (625ml) canned pineapple juice, frozen
250g strawberries, halved
2 cups crushed ice
1 cup (250ml) sparkling mineral water

Blend or process ingredients, in batches,
until almost smooth. Combine batches in large jug.

per serving 0.6g fat; 507kJ (121 cal)

lime and ginger ceviche

PREPARATION TIME 20 MINUTES (PLUS REFRIGERATION TIME)

Ceviche is a centuries-old Latin American dish using citrus juice to "cook" raw seafood. We used kingfish fillets in our recipe, but you can use whatever you prefer – just be certain to buy the freshest sashimi fish you can find because, while the citrus juice changes the colour and texture, the fish in this recipe has not been cooked with heat. You need about 10 limes for this recipe.

24 scallops (600g),
   roe removed
400g piece sashimi kingfish,
   sliced thinly
¼ cup finely grated lime rind
1½ teaspoons sea salt
1 teaspoon cracked
   black pepper
4 green onions, sliced thinly
2 tablespoons grated
   fresh ginger
4 kaffir lime leaves,
   shredded finely
1 cup (250ml) lime juice

1 Split scallops in half through centre. Place in large shallow dish with remaining ingredients; toss to coat seafood in marinade. Spread evenly in dish to ensure seafood is submerged in marinade. Cover; refrigerate, stirring occasionally, about 1½ hours or until seafood softens and is almost opaque.
2 Divide ceviche among serving plates; serve with slices of crusty bread and lime wedges, if desired.

serves 4
per serving 3.2g fat;
744kJ (178 cal)

steak tartare

PREPARATION TIME 40 MINUTES

Buy the freshest beef available; it is always a good idea to check with your butcher to find out if the meat you purchased can be eaten raw. It is very important to keep the beef as cold as possible when preparing this recipe. Use a sharp knife to chop the beef so that it neither tears nor becomes overly minced.

600g piece beef eye
    fillet, trimmed
2 cloves garlic, crushed
1 tablespoon dijon mustard
½ teaspoon Tabasco sauce
1 teaspoon worcestershire
    sauce
4 quail eggs
1 small red onion (100g),
    chopped finely
1 tablespoon drained capers,
    rinsed, chopped finely
4 anchovy fillets,
    chopped finely
¼ cup finely chopped
    fresh flat-leaf parsley

1 Chop beef finely; combine beef in large chilled bowl with garlic, mustard and sauces. Divide tartare mixture among serving plates, making a small well in the centre of each mound.

2 Crack one egg carefully into each well. Divide onion, capers, anchovy and parsley among serving plates; serve immediately.

serves 4
per serving 7.1g fat;
896kJ (214 cal)

SERVING SUGGESTION
Serve with toasted slices of
a french stick.

smoothies and lassies

Each of these smoothies and lassies can be prepared in about 15 minutes; each serves 4 and makes 2 litres.

berry smoothie

500g frozen mixed berries
2¼ cups (600g) frozen vanilla yogurt
1 litre (4 cups) raspberry lemonade, chilled

Blend or process ingredients, in batches, until smooth; strain through fine sieve into large jug. Stir to combine.

per serving 5.2g fat; 1277kJ (305 cal)

cranberry smoothie

1 litre (4 cups) cranberry juice, chilled
3 large bananas (700g), halved
2 cups (500ml) no-fat milk

Blend or process ingredients, in batches, until smooth. Combine batches in large jug.

per serving 0.8g fat; 901kJ (215 cal)

mango lassie

3 large mangoes (1.5kg), chopped coarsely
2⅔ cups (750g) yogurt
3 cups crushed ice
1 cup (250ml) water

Blend or process ingredients, in batches,
until smooth. Combine batches in large jug.

per serving 6.9g fat; 1198kJ (286 cal)

apple and melon lassie

700g honeydew melon, chopped coarsely
2 cups (500ml) clear apple juice
500g yogurt
2 cups crushed ice
½ cup firmly packed fresh mint leaves
4cm piece fresh ginger (20g), grated
1 cup (250ml) water

Blend or process ingredients, in batches, until almost smooth.
Combine batches in large jug.

per serving 4.9g fat; 791kJ (189 cal)

nam jim chicken

PREPARATION TIME 20 MINUTES **COOKING TIME** 20 MINUTES

When removing coriander leaves from stalks, save the root part from one of the stalks for the nam jim sauce.

8 chicken thigh fillets (880g)
1 teaspoon ground cumin
1 teaspoon ground coriander
2 tablespoons grated palm sugar
1 cup loosely packed fresh thai basil leaves
1 cup loosely packed fresh coriander leaves
3 cups (240g) bean sprouts

NAM JIM SAUCE
3 long green chillies, seeded, chopped coarsely
2 cloves garlic, quartered
10cm piece fresh lemon grass, sliced thinly
3 green onions, chopped coarsely
1 coriander root, chopped coarsely
¼ cup (60ml) lime juice
1 tablespoon fish sauce
2 tablespoons grated palm sugar

1 Combine chicken in large bowl with cumin, coriander and sugar; toss to coat chicken in spice mixture.
2 Cook chicken in heated lightly oiled large non-stick frying pan, in batches, until browned all over and cooked through.
3 Meanwhile, make nam jim sauce.
4 Serve chicken on combined herbs and sprouts; top with sauce.
NAM JIM SAUCE Blend or process ingredients until smooth.

serves 4
per serving 14g fat; 1636kJ (391 cal)

sang choy bow

PREPARATION TIME 15 MINUTES **COOKING TIME** 15 MINUTES

2 teaspoons sesame oil
500g lean pork mince
1 small brown onion (80g),
   chopped finely
1 clove garlic, crushed
1cm piece fresh ginger
   (5g), grated
2 tablespoons water
100g shiitake mushrooms,
   chopped finely
2 tablespoons soy sauce
2 tablespoons oyster sauce
1 tablespoon lime juice
2 cups (160g) bean sprouts
4 green onions, sliced thinly
¼ cup coarsely chopped
   fresh coriander
12 large butter lettuce leaves

1 Heat oil in wok or large frying
   pan; stir-fry pork, brown onion,
   garlic and ginger until pork is just
   changed in colour.
2 Add the water, mushrooms,
   sauces and juice; stir-fry until
   mushrooms are just tender.
   Remove from heat, add sprouts,
   green onion and coriander; toss
   gently to combine.
3 Divide lettuce leaves among
   serving plates; spoon sang choy
   bow into leaves.

serves 4
per serving 11.4g fat;
1021kJ (244 cal)

stir-fried seafood with chilli and ginger

PREPARATION TIME 20 MINUTES **COOKING TIME** 20 MINUTES

300g squid hoods
300g uncooked medium
  king prawns
500g large black mussels
1½ cups (300g) jasmine rice
2 teaspoons sesame oil
4cm piece fresh ginger
  (20g), grated
1 tablespoon sambal oelek
250g cleaned baby octopus
350g bok choy,
  chopped coarsely
400g gai larn,
  chopped coarsely
¼ cup (60ml) kecap manis
4 fresh kaffir lime leaves,
  shredded finely

1 Cut squid down centre to open out, score inside in diagonal pattern then cut into strips. Shell and devein prawns, leaving tails intact. Scrub mussels under cold water; discard beards.

2 Cook rice in large saucepan of boiling water, uncovered, until just tender; drain. Cover to keep warm.

3 Meanwhile, heat oil in wok or large frying pan; stir-fry ginger, sambal and seafood, in batches, until seafood changes colour and mussels open (discard any that do not).

4 Return all seafood to wok. Add bok choy, gai larn and kecap manis; stir-fry until vegetables just wilt. Remove from heat; stir in lime leaves. Serve with rice.

serves 4
per serving 4.7g fat;
1854kJ (442 cal)

57

stir-fried prawns with pineapple and chilli salad

PREPARATION TIME 25 MINUTES **COOKING TIME** 10 MINUTES

1.5kg uncooked large king prawns
1 clove garlic, crushed
2cm piece fresh ginger (10g), grated
4 green onions, sliced thinly
1 tablespoon sesame oil

PINEAPPLE AND CHILLI SALAD
1 small fresh pineapple (800g)
2 medium mangoes (860g)
¼ cup (30g) coarsely chopped toasted peanuts
1 fresh long red chilli, sliced thinly
2 green onions, sliced thinly
1 tablespoon finely chopped fresh vietnamese mint
¼ cup finely chopped fresh coriander
2 tablespoons lime juice
1 tablespoon fish sauce
2 teaspoons sugar

1 Shell and devein prawns, leaving tails intact. Place in medium bowl with garlic, ginger and onion; toss gently to combine.
2 Make pineapple and chilli salad.
3 Heat oil in wok or large frying pan; stir-fry prawn mixture until prawns are just changed in colour.
4 Divide salad among serving plates; top with prawns.
PINEAPPLE AND CHILLI SALAD Slice pineapple and mango thinly; cut slices into 5mm matchsticks. Combine fruit in large bowl with nuts, chilli, onion and herbs. Place juice, sauce and sugar in screw-top jar; shake well. Add dressing to salad; toss gently to combine.

serves 4
per serving 9.8g fat; 1648kJ (394 cal)

light-white frittata

PREPARATION TIME 15 MINUTES **COOKING TIME** 20 MINUTES

You need 200g of fresh peas
in their pods for this recipe.

½ cup (80g) fresh shelled peas
1 medium yellow capsicum
    (200g), sliced thinly
1 small kumara (250g),
    grated coarsely
12 egg whites
½ cup (120g) light sour cream
1 cup loosely packed fresh
    basil leaves
¼ cup (20g) finely grated
    parmesan cheese

1 Cook peas, capsicum and
   kumara in heated lightly oiled
   20cm non-stick frying pan,
   stirring, until just tender.
2 Whisk egg whites and cream
   in medium bowl; stir in basil.
3 Pour egg-white mixture over
   vegetables; cook, covered, over
   low heat about 10 minutes or
   until frittata is almost set.
4 Sprinkle cheese over frittata;
   place under preheated grill
   until frittata is set and top is
   browned lightly.

serves 4
per serving 7.6g fat;
742kJ (177 cal)

TIPS Frittata can be served
hot or at room temperature.
You can freeze the yolks, in
packages of two or four, for
future use when baking or
when making custard.
Fresh peas can be substituted
with frozen peas, if you prefer.

lemon and rosemary veal cutlets

PREPARATION TIME 20 MINUTES (PLUS REFRIGERATION TIME) **COOKING TIME** 25 MINUTES

1 tablespoon finely chopped
   fresh rosemary

2 tablespoons finely grated
   lemon rind

2 tablespoons olive oil

4 x 200g veal chops, trimmed

1kg kipfler potatoes

2 tablespoons lemon juice

1 clove garlic, crushed

8 red radishes (280g),
   sliced thinly

4 green onions, sliced thinly

1 Combine rosemary, rind and oil in small jug; stand 10 minutes. Place half of the marinade in medium bowl with veal; toss to coat veal in marinade. Cover; refrigerate 3 hours or overnight.

2 Boil, steam or microwave unpeeled potatoes until just tender; drain. Quarter potatoes lengthways.

3 Stir juice and garlic into reserved remaining marinade.

4 Cook veal in heated lightly oiled large non-stick frying pan until browned both sides and cooked as desired.

5 Meanwhile, place potato, radish and onion in large bowl; toss salad gently to combine. Serve veal on salad; drizzle with reserved marinade mixture.

serves 4
per serving 12.4g fat;
1579kJ (377 cal)

beef fillet with gremolata and semi-dried tomato polenta

PREPARATION TIME 15 MINUTES (PLUS REFRIGERATION TIME) **COOKING TIME** 25 MINUTES

1½ cups (375ml) water
1½ cups (375ml) prepared vegetable stock
¾ cup (120g) polenta
⅓ cup (75g) semi-dried tomatoes, chopped coarsely
2 tablespoons finely grated parmesan cheese
500g piece beef eye fillet

GREMOLATA
½ cup coarsely chopped fresh flat-leaf parsley
¼ cup (60ml) lemon juice
1 tablespoon finely grated lemon rind
1 clove garlic, crushed

1 Lightly oil 23cm-square cake pan.
2 Combine the water and stock in large saucepan; bring to a boil. Gradually add polenta to liquid, stirring constantly. Reduce heat; cook, stirring constantly, about 10 minutes or until polenta thickens. Stir in tomato and cheese; spread polenta into prepared pan. Cover; refrigerate about 1 hour or until firm.
3 Meanwhile, make gremolata.
4 Cook beef in heated lightly oiled large non-stick frying pan until browned all over and cooked as desired. Cover; stand 10 minutes then slice thickly.
5 Meanwhile, turn polenta onto board; cut into four squares, cut each square diagonally into two triangles. Cook polenta triangles in same pan, in batches, until browned lightly both sides.
6 Divide polenta among serving plates; top with beef then gremolata.
GREMOLATA Combine ingredients in small bowl.

serves 4
per serving 7.6g fat; 1359kJ (325 cal)

pappardelle with balmain bugs

PREPARATION TIME 25 MINUTES **COOKING TIME** 15 MINUTES

Since most balmain bugs are sold already cooked, you may have to ask your fishmonger to order uncooked bugs for you for this recipe; uncooked moreton bay bugs can be substituted.

18 uncooked balmain
   bugs (3.6kg)
1 tablespoon finely grated
   lemon rind
⅓ cup (80ml) lemon juice
1 teaspoon dijon mustard
1 tablespoon olive oil
375g pappardelle
½ cup coarsely chopped
   fresh basil
½ cup coarsely chopped fresh
   flat-leaf parsley
4 green onions, sliced thinly

1 Place bugs upside-down on chopping board; cut tail from body, discard body. Halve tail lengthways; discard back vein.
2 Combine rind, juice, mustard and oil in large bowl.
3 Cook pasta in large saucepan of boiling water, uncovered, until just tender; drain.
4 Meanwhile, cook bugs, in batches, on heated lightly oiled grill plate (or grill or barbecue) until just changed in colour.
5 Add pasta and bugs to rind mixture in bowl with herbs and onion; toss gently to combine.

serves 4
per serving 5.7g fat;
1556kJ (372 cal)

pepper-crusted swordfish with bean and potato salad

PREPARATION TIME 15 MINUTES **COOKING TIME** 15 MINUTES

300g small red-skinned
   potatoes, halved
¼ cup (60ml) lime juice
1 tablespoon olive oil
1 clove garlic, crushed
1 teaspoon ground
   white pepper
2 teaspoons cracked
   black pepper
½ cup (35g) stale breadcrumbs
4 x 200g swordfish fillets
200g green beans
200g yellow beans

1 Boil, steam or microwave potato until just tender; drain. Cover to keep warm.
2 Meanwhile, place juice, oil and garlic in screw-top jar; shake well. Combine peppers and breadcrumbs in small bowl.
3 Press pepper mixture onto one side of each fish fillet. Cook fish, crumbed-side down, in heated lightly oiled large non-stick frying pan, until browned lightly and crisp; turn, cook until browned lightly and cooked as desired.
4 Meanwhile, boil, steam or microwave beans until just tender; drain.
5 Place potato and beans in large bowl with dressing; toss gently to combine. Serve fish with salad.

serves 4
per serving 9.5g fat;
1404kJ (335 cal)

beef and noodle salad

PREPARATION TIME 15 MINUTES **COOKING TIME** 10 MINUTES

Bean thread noodles, also known as wun sen, glass or cellophane noodles, are made from mung beans. These delicate, fine noodles must be softened in boiling water before use; after soaking, they become transparent.

400g beef eye fillet steaks
2 tablespoons soy sauce
1 tablespoon sesame oil
250g bean thread noodles
1 medium red onion (170g), sliced thinly
1 large carrot (180g), sliced thinly
1 lebanese cucumber (130g), seeded, sliced thinly
½ cup loosely packed fresh coriander leaves
¼ cup coarsely chopped fresh thai basil
¼ cup (60ml) lime juice
¼ cup (60ml) sweet chilli sauce
2 tablespoons fish sauce

1 Combine beef, soy sauce and half of the oil in medium bowl; toss to coat beef in marinade.
2 Meanwhile, place noodles in large heatproof bowl, cover with boiling water, stand until just tender; drain. Rinse under cold water; drain.
3 Combine noodles in large bowl with onion, carrot, cucumber and herbs. Combine juice, sauces and remaining oil in small jug.
4 Drain beef; discard marinade. Cook beef in heated lightly oiled medium non-stick frying pan until browned both sides and cooked as desired. Cover; stand 10 minutes then slice thinly. Add beef and dressing to salad; toss gently to combine. Serve with lime wedges, if desired.

serves 4
per serving 10.2g fat; 1187kJ (284 cal)

chicken and mixed pea stir-fry

PREPARATION TIME 15 MINUTES **COOKING TIME** 20 MINUTES

Char siu sauce is a chinese barbecue sauce based on soy beans; it is available from most supermarkets.

1½ cups (300g) jasmine rice
1 tablespoon peanut oil
700g chicken breast fillets, sliced thinly
1 medium brown onion (150g), sliced thinly
1 fresh long red chilli, seeded, sliced thinly
1 clove garlic, crushed
150g sugar snap peas, trimmed
150g snow peas, trimmed
125g fresh baby corn, halved
2 tablespoons kecap manis
2 tablespoons char siu sauce
½ cup (125ml) prepared chicken stock
1 tablespoon cornflour
2 tablespoons lime juice

1 Cook rice in large saucepan of boiling water, uncovered, until just tender; drain. Cover to keep warm.
2 Meanwhile, heat half of the oil in wok or large frying pan; stir-fry chicken, in batches, until browned and almost cooked through.
3 Heat remaining oil in same wok; stir-fry onion, chilli and garlic until onion softens. Add peas and corn; stir-fry until vegetables are just tender. Return chicken to wok with sauces and stock; stir-fry about 2 minutes or until chicken is cooked through. Stir in blended cornflour and juice; stir-fry until sauce boils and thickens. Divide rice among serving plates; top with stir-fry.

serves 4
per serving 9.7g fat; 2487kJ (594 cal)

cajun prawns with bean and coriander salad

PREPARATION TIME 30 MINUTES **COOKING TIME** 15 MINUTES

You need three limes for this recipe.

1 tablespoon hot paprika
1 teaspoon chilli powder
1 teaspoon ground ginger
2 teaspoons ground cumin
1 teaspoon ground cardamom
1 teaspoon ground coriander
1 tablespoon vegetable oil
1 medium red onion (150g), chopped coarsely
1 clove garlic, crushed
24 uncooked medium king prawns (1kg)
1 teaspoon vegetable oil, extra
1 tablespoon lime juice
1 lime, cut into wedges

BEAN AND CORIANDER SALAD

400g green beans, halved crossways
1 cup loosely packed fresh coriander leaves
4 small vine-ripened tomatoes (120g), quartered
1 medium red onion (150g), sliced thinly
1 teaspoon coarsely grated lime rind
2 tablespoons lime juice
1 clove garlic, crushed
1 teaspoon sugar

1 Blend or process spices, oil, onion and garlic until mixture forms a paste. Shell and devein prawns, leaving tails intact.
2 Make bean and coriander salad.
3 Heat extra oil in wok or large frying pan; stir-fry prawns, in batches, until just changed in colour.
4 Cook paste, stirring, in same wok about 2 minutes or until fragrant. Return prawns to wok with juice; stir-fry until prawns are heated through. Serve prawns with salad and lime wedges.
   BEAN AND CORIANDER SALAD Boil, steam or microwave beans until just tender; drain. Rinse under cold water; drain. Combine beans in medium bowl with coriander, tomato and onion. Whisk rind, juice, garlic and sugar in small jug to combine. Pour dressing over salad; toss gently to combine.

serves 4
per serving 15.8g fat; 863kJ (206 cal)

chinese-spiced chicken

PREPARATION TIME 20 MINUTES **COOKING TIME** 20 MINUTES

You need a 20cm-square piece of clean, dry cotton muslin to make our bouquet garni, the classic French bag of dried spices often used to infuse stocks and sauces.

1 tablespoon peanut oil
6 green onions, chopped finely
2cm piece fresh ginger
   (10g), grated
1 clove garlic, crushed
2 tablespoons soy sauce
2 tablespoons dry sherry
1 teaspoon toasted
   sesame seeds
700g chicken breast fillets
375g fresh thin egg noodles

BOUQUET GARNI
2 star anise
1 cinnamon stick, crushed
1 teaspoon fennel seeds
3 whole cloves

1 Heat oil in small saucepan; cook onion, ginger and garlic, stirring, 1 minute. Add soy sauce, sherry and seeds; simmer, stirring, 1 minute. Remove from heat; reserve.

2 Make bouquet garni. Place bouquet garni and chicken in large saucepan of boiling water; return to a boil. Reduce heat; simmer, stirring occasionally, about 10 minutes or until chicken is cooked through. Cool chicken in poaching liquid 10 minutes. Remove chicken from pan then slice thinly. Discard bouquet garni.

3 Return poaching liquid in pan to a boil; cook noodles, uncovered, until just tender. Drain noodles, reserving 2 tablespoons of the poaching liquid; stir the liquid through noodles in large bowl. Divide noodles among serving bowls; top with chicken and onion mixture. BOUQUET GARNI Place ingredients in centre of 20cm muslin square; bring four corners together, tie together tightly with cotton kitchen string.

serves 4
per serving 10.1g fat; 2101kJ (502 cal)

poached eggs and asparagus with dill sauce

PREPARATION TIME 5 MINUTES **COOKING TIME** 20 MINUTES

20g butter
¼ teaspoon saffron threads
1 teaspoon dijon mustard
1 tablespoon plain flour
1 cup (250ml) prepared
   salt-reduced vegetable stock
2 tablespoons finely chopped
   fresh dill
750g asparagus, trimmed
4 eggs

1 Melt butter with saffron in small
   saucepan over medium heat;
   stir in mustard. Add flour; cook,
   stirring, until mixture thickens
   and bubbles. Gradually add
   stock; stir until mixture boils
   and thickens. Stir in dill.

2 Boil, steam or microwave
   asparagus until just tender,
   drain; cover to keep warm.

3 Half-fill a large shallow frying
   pan with water; bring to a boil.
   Break eggs into cup then slide
   into pan, one at a time. When all
   eggs are in pan, allow water to
   return to a boil. Cover pan, turn
   off heat; stand about 4 minutes
   or until a light film of egg white
   sets over yolks. Using egg slide,
   remove eggs, one at a time, and
   place on absorbent-paper-lined
   saucer to blot up poaching liquid.

4 Divide asparagus among serving
   bowls; top with eggs, drizzle with
   dill sauce.

serves 4
per serving 9.8g fat;
658kJ (157 cal)

lemon-fetta couscous with steamed vegetables

PREPARATION TIME 20 MINUTES **COOKING TIME** 10 MINUTES

You need about half a butternut pumpkin for this recipe. Preserved lemons, a North African specialty, are quartered and preserved in salt and lemon juice. To use, remove and discard pulp, squeeze juice from rind, rinse rind well then use. Sold in jars or in bulk by delicatessens; once opened, store preserved lemon in the refrigerator.

600g butternut pumpkin,
    chopped coarsely
2 small green zucchini (180g),
    chopped coarsely
2 small yellow zucchini (180g),
    chopped coarsely
300g spinach, trimmed,
    chopped coarsely
2 cups (500ml) prepared
    vegetable stock
2 cups (400g) couscous
¼ cup (60ml) lemon juice
⅓ cup coarsely chopped
    fresh basil
200g low-fat fetta cheese,
    chopped coarsely
¼ cup (50g) finely chopped
    preserved lemon rind
6 green onions, sliced thinly

1 Boil, steam or microwave pumpkin, green and yellow zucchini and spinach, separately, until tender; drain.

2 Meanwhile, bring stock to a boil in large saucepan. Add couscous, remove from heat, cover; stand about 5 minutes or until liquid is absorbed, fluffing with fork occasionally. Place couscous and vegetables in large bowl with remaining ingredients; toss gently to combine.

serves 4
per serving 9.4g fat;
2427kJ (581 cal)

citrus-ginger steamed bream

PREPARATION TIME 20 MINUTES **COOKING TIME** 15 MINUTES

We used whole bream for this recipe, but any fairly small white-fleshed fish can be used. You need four 80cm-long sheets of foil to wrap the fish.

1 medium lemon (140g)
2 medium oranges (480g)
2 cloves garlic, crushed
2cm piece fresh ginger (10g), grated
4 x 250g whole bream, cleaned
2 cups (400g) jasmine rice
⅓ cup loosely packed fresh basil leaves, torn

1 Using vegetable peeler, peel rind carefully from lemon and one orange; cut rind into thin strips. Squeeze juice of both oranges and lemon into large bowl. Stir in rind, garlic and ginger. Score fish both sides; add to bowl, coat in marinade.
2 Fold 80cm-long piece of foil in half crossways; place one fish on foil, spoon a quarter of the marinade onto fish. Fold foil over fish to tightly enclose. Repeat process with remaining fish and marinade.
3 Place fish parcels in large steamer fitted over large saucepan of boiling water; steam, covered, about 15 minutes or until cooked as desired.
4 Meanwhile, cook rice in large saucepan of boiling water, uncovered, until just tender; drain. Divide rice among serving plates; top with fish, drizzle with cooking juices, sprinkle with basil.

serves 4
per serving 7.6g fat; 2376kJ (568 cal)

TIP Use a zester, if you have one, to remove orange and lemon rind.

chicken gow gees

PREPARATION TIME 30 MINUTES (PLUS REFRIGERATION TIME)
COOKING TIME 10 MINUTES

Gow gee wrappers are found packaged in the refrigerated section
of Asian grocery stores as well as in some supermarkets. Wonton
or spring roll wrappers can be used instead.

400g lean chicken mince
2 green onions, chopped finely
2 cloves garlic, crushed
2cm piece fresh ginger (10g), grated
¼ teaspoon five-spice powder
½ cup (50g) packaged breadcrumbs
1 tablespoon hoisin sauce
2 tablespoons coarsely chopped fresh coriander
1 tablespoon coarsely chopped fresh thai basil
1 egg
24 gow gee wrappers

SWEET CHILLI DIPPING SAUCE
⅓ cup (80ml) sweet chilli sauce
¼ cup (60ml) red wine vinegar
¼ cup coarsely chopped fresh coriander

1 Using hand, combine chicken, onion, garlic, ginger, five-spice,
   breadcrumbs, sauce, herbs and egg in large bowl. Roll level
   tablespoons of the mixture into balls; place balls on tray. Cover;
   refrigerate 30 minutes.
2 Meanwhile, make sweet chilli dipping sauce.
3 Brush one wrapper with water; place one chicken ball in centre of
   wrapper. Fold wrapper over to completely enclose chicken ball. Pleat
   edge of wrapper along join; repeat process with remaining wrappers
   and chicken balls.
4 Place gow gees, in single layer, about 1cm apart in baking-paper lined
   steamer fitted over large saucepan of boiling water; steam, covered,
   about 8 minutes or until gow gees are cooked through.
   SWEET CHILLI DIPPING SAUCE Place ingredients in screw-top jar;
   shake well.

serves 4
per serving 7.3g fat; 1315kJ (314 cal)

vine-leaf-wrapped swordfish with tomato-olive salsa

PREPARATION TIME 20 MINUTES **COOKING TIME** 20 MINUTES

16 large fresh grapevine leaves
4 x 200g swordfish steaks

TOMATO-OLIVE SALSA
3 cloves garlic, crushed
1 cup loosely packed fresh flat-leaf parsley leaves
¼ cup coarsely chopped fresh chives
3 small tomatoes (390g), chopped coarsely
½ cup (75g) seeded kalamata olives, quartered lengthways
2 tablespoons drained capers, rinsed
2 tablespoons lemon juice
2 teaspoons olive oil

1 Trim vine leaves; using metal tongs, dip, one at a time, in medium saucepan of boiling salted water. Rinse immediately under cold water; drain on absorbent paper.
2 Overlap four vine leaves slightly to form a rectangle large enough to wrap each piece of fish; fold leaves around fish to enclose completely. Place fish parcels in large steamer fitted over large saucepan of boiling water; steam, covered, about 15 minutes or until cooked as desired.
3 Meanwhile, make tomato-olive salsa.
4 Place fish parcels on serving bowls; pull back vine leaves to uncover fish, top with salsa.
TOMATO-OLIVE SALSA Combine ingredients in medium bowl.

serves 4
per serving 3.7g fat; 453kJ (108 cal)

TIP If you are unable to find fresh grapevine leaves, buy those that come cryovac-packed in brine; they can be found in most Greek or Middle-Eastern food stores. Be sure to rinse them in cold water and dry with absorbent paper before using.

chicken and fresh pea risoni

PREPARATION TIME 15 MINUTES **COOKING TIME** 30 MINUTES

Risoni is a small rice-shaped pasta very similar to orzo.
You need 400g of fresh peas in their pods for this recipe.

400g chicken breast fillets
1 litre (4 cups) prepared
  chicken stock
300g sugar snap peas, trimmed
1 cup (160g) fresh shelled peas
1 tablespoon olive oil
1 small leek (200g), sliced thinly
1 clove garlic, crushed
500g risoni
½ cup (125ml) dry white wine
1 tablespoon white
  wine vinegar
1 tablespoon finely chopped
  fresh tarragon

1 Combine chicken and stock
  in medium frying pan; bring to
  a boil. Reduce heat; simmer,
  uncovered, about 10 minutes
  or until cooked through. Cool
  chicken in poaching liquid
  10 minutes. Remove chicken
  from pan; reserve stock. Slice
  chicken thinly.
2 Meanwhile, boil, steam or
  microwave peas, separately,
  until just tender; drain.
3 Heat oil in large saucepan; cook
  leek and garlic, stirring, until leek
  softens. Add risoni; stir to coat
  in leek mixture. Add wine; stir
  until wine is almost absorbed.
  Add reserved stock; bring to
  a boil. Reduce heat; simmer,
  uncovered, stirring occasionally,
  until stock is absorbed and risoni
  is just tender. Stir in vinegar;
  remove from heat. Gently stir
  in chicken, peas and tarragon.

serves 4
per serving 9.7g fat;
2862kJ (684 cal)

herbed ricotta ravioli in tomato broth

PREPARATION TIME 20 MINUTES (PLUS REFRIGERATION TIME) **COOKING TIME** 10 MINUTES

⅓ cup (30g) finely grated
  parmesan cheese
⅔ cup (130g) low-fat
  ricotta cheese
1 tablespoon finely
  chopped fresh basil
2 tablespoons finely
  chopped fresh chives
24 wonton wrappers
16 medium egg
  tomatoes (1.2kg)
2 green onions, sliced thinly

1 Combine cheeses and herbs in small bowl. Place one rounded teaspoon of cheese mixture in centre of each of 12 wonton wrappers; brush around edge with a little water. Top each with a remaining wrapper, press around edges firmly to seal. Place ravioli on tray, cover; refrigerate 20 minutes.

2 Meanwhile, bring large saucepan of water to a boil. Place cored tomatoes in pan; return to a boil. Cook, uncovered, 2 minutes. Strain tomatoes over large bowl; reserve cooking liquid.

3 Blend or process tomatoes, in batches, until smooth; push through a food mill (mouli) or sieve into small saucepan; bring to a boil. Reduce heat; simmer broth, uncovered, 5 minutes.

4 Meanwhile, cook ravioli in large saucepan of reserved cooking liquid, uncovered, about 4 minutes or until ravioli float to the surface; discard cooking liquid. Divide tomato broth and ravioli among serving bowls; sprinkle with onion.

serves 4
per serving 5.9g fat;
850kJ (203 cal)

mexican beef salad with fresh corn salsa

PREPARATION TIME 25 MINUTES **COOKING TIME** 20 MINUTES

Chipotle are what fresh jalapeño chillies are called after they've been dried and smoked. Having a deep, intensely smoky flavour rather than a searing heat, chipotles are dark brown, almost black in appearance; they are available from specialty spice stores and gourmet delicatessens. You need four cobs of corn for this recipe.

4 dried chipotle chillies
⅓ cup (80ml) boiling water
1 medium red onion (150g), chopped coarsely
2 cups (500ml) water, extra
1 tablespoon ground cumin
1 cup (250ml) prepared beef stock
300g piece beef eye fillet, cut into 3mm slices
2 tablespoons light sour cream
½ cup coarsely chopped fresh coriander

FRESH CORN SALSA
1 medium red onion (150g), chopped coarsely
4 cups (660g) fresh corn kernels
2 cloves garlic, crushed
⅓ cup (80ml) lime juice
3 long green chillies, sliced thinly
1 small avocado (200g), chopped coarsely

1 Soak chillies in the boiling water in small heatproof bowl for 10 minutes. When cool enough to handle, remove stalks from chillies; reserve chillies and liquid.

2 Meanwhile, make fresh corn salsa.

3 Cook onion in lightly oiled large frying pan, stirring, until soft. Add the extra water, cumin, stock, chillies and reserved liquid; bring to a boil. Reduce heat; simmer, uncovered, 10 minutes. Using slotted spoon, remove solids from chilli poaching liquid; reserve.

4 Place beef, in single layer, in chilli poaching liquid; turn off heat. Turn beef over; using slotted spoon, remove beef from liquid after 30 seconds. Cover to keep warm.

5 Blend or process reserved solids with cream until almost smooth. Serve beef on salsa; top with chilli cream sauce and sprinkle with coriander. FRESH CORN SALSA Combine ingredients in medium bowl.

serves 4
per serving 15g fat; 1564kJ (374 cal)

TIP The strained beef and chilli poaching liquid can be kept, covered, in the refrigerator or freezer, then used at a later date to impart its distinctive flavour to soups or sauces.
SERVING SUGGESTION Serve with warmed flour tortillas, if desired.

meatball pho

PREPARATION TIME 20 MINUTES **COOKING TIME** 15 MINUTES

Pho, the well-known vietnamese noodle soup, is usually eaten for breakfast, but we like to eat it any time of the day.

400g lean beef mince
2 tablespoons finely chopped fresh lemon grass
2 green onions, chopped finely
1 clove garlic, crushed
1 egg white
1½ litres (6 cups) prepared beef stock
2 star anise
1 stick cinnamon
185g dried rice stick noodles
1 cup (80g) bean sprouts
1 cup loosely packed fresh coriander leaves
2 fresh long red chillies, sliced thinly
4 green onions, sliced thinly

1 Using hand, combine beef, lemon grass, chopped onion, garlic and egg white in medium bowl; roll level tablespoons of the mixture into balls.

2 Heat stock, star anise and cinnamon in large saucepan; bring to a boil. Reduce heat; simmer, uncovered, 5 minutes. Add meatballs; return to a boil. Reduce heat; simmer, uncovered, about 5 minutes or until meatballs are cooked through. Discard star anise and cinnamon from pan.

3 Meanwhile, place noodles in large heatproof bowl, cover with boiling water, stand until just tender; drain.

4 Divide noodles, meatballs and stock among serving bowls; top with combined sprouts, coriander, chilli and sliced onion. Serve with lime wedges, if desired.

serves 4
per serving 8.4g fat; 1399kJ (334 cal)

gourmet chicken sandwiches

PREPARATION TIME 20 MINUTES **COOKING TIME** 15 MINUTES

Black cumin seeds, also sold as jeera kala, are darker and sweeter than ordinary cumin and are sometimes confused with kalonji (nigella seeds). Used extensively in Indian and Moroccan-style cooking, the nutty flavour of black cumin seeds is brought out by toasting.

600g chicken breast fillets
2 cups (500ml) prepared
   chicken stock
1½ cups (375ml) water
⅓ cup (50g) drained
   sun-dried tomatoes
1 tablespoon coarsely
   chopped fresh rosemary
2 tablespoons prepared
   chicken stock, extra
½ long loaf pide
½ small red onion (50g),
   sliced thinly
1 lebanese cucumber (130g),
   sliced thinly
60g baby rocket leaves
⅓ cup (95g) yogurt
½ teaspoon toasted black
   cumin seeds

1 Combine chicken, stock and the water in large saucepan; bring to a boil. Reduce heat; simmer, uncovered, about 10 minutes or until cooked through. Cool chicken in poaching liquid 10 minutes. Remove chicken from pan; discard poaching liquid (or reserve for another use). Slice chicken thinly.
2 Meanwhile, drain tomatoes on absorbent paper; pressing firmly to remove as much oil as possible. Quarter tomatoes; blend or process with rosemary and extra stock until tomato mixture forms a paste.
3 Halve pide, slice pieces horizontally; toast both sides. Spread cut sides of pide with tomato paste; top with chicken, onion, cucumber and rocket. Serve with combined yogurt and seeds.

serves 4
per serving 8.4g fat; 1720kJ (411 cal)

chicken breasts poached with ham and herbs

PREPARATION TIME 30 MINUTES **COOKING TIME** 15 MINUTES

4 x 170g single chicken breast fillets
¼ cup finely chopped fresh chives
¼ cup finely chopped fresh basil
2 cloves garlic, crushed
2 teaspoons finely grated lemon rind
1 teaspoon olive oil
200g thinly sliced leg ham
4 green onions, sliced thinly

LEMON MUSTARD DRESSING
3 teaspoons olive oil
¼ cup (60ml) lemon juice
1 teaspoon dijon mustard

1 Pound chicken between sheets of plastic wrap until 1cm thick. Combine herbs, garlic, rind and oil in small bowl. Divide herb mixture among chicken fillets; top with ham.
2 Starting from one long side, roll chicken pieces tightly; enclose in plastic wrap, twisting ends to seal. Enclose each roll in one more layer of plastic wrap to secure.
3 Bring large frying pan of water to a boil; add rolls. Reduce heat; simmer, covered, about 15 minutes or until chicken is cooked through. Remove rolls from poaching liquid; cool rolls 5 minutes. Discard poaching liquid.
4 Meanwhile, make lemon mustard dressing.
5 Remove plastic wrap; slice rolls thinly. Divide slices among serving bowls; sprinkle with onion, drizzle with dressing and serve with steamed green beans, if desired.
LEMON MUSTARD DRESSING Place ingredients in screw-top jar; shake well.

serves 4
per serving 10.4g fat; 1234kJ (295 cal)

scallops with sugar snap pea salad

PREPARATION TIME 20 MINUTES **COOKING TIME** 5 MINUTES

250g sugar snap peas, trimmed
20 scallops on the half shell (800g), roe removed
100g cherry tomatoes, halved
1 medium lebanese cucumber (130g), seeded, sliced thinly
½ cup loosely packed fresh mint leaves

BALSAMIC DRESSING
1 teaspoon finely grated lemon rind
2 tablespoons lemon juice
1 clove garlic, crushed
1 tablespoon olive oil
2 teaspoons balsamic vinegar

LEMON DRESSING
1 tablespoon finely grated lemon rind
¼ cup (60ml) lemon juice
1 clove garlic, crushed
1 tablespoon olive oil

1 Make balsamic dressing. Make lemon dressing.
2 Boil, steam or microwave peas until just tender; drain.
3 Remove scallops from shell; reserve shells. Place scallops, in single layer,
   in large steamer fitted over large saucepan of boiling water; steam scallops,
   covered, about 4 minutes or until cooked as desired.
4 Meanwhile, rinse and dry scallop shells.
5 Place peas in medium bowl with tomato, cucumber, mint and balsamic
   dressing; toss gently to combine.
6 Return scallops to shells; drizzle with lemon dressing. Serve scallops with salad.
   BALSAMIC DRESSING Place ingredients in screw-top jar; shake well.
   LEMON DRESSING Place ingredients in screw-top jar; shake well.

serves 4
per serving 10.6g fat; 965kJ (231 cal)

mussels with asian flavours

PREPARATION TIME 20 MINUTES **COOKING TIME** 15 MINUTES

1.5kg black mussels
1¼ cups (250g) jasmine rice
1 tablespoon sesame oil
4cm piece fresh ginger
  (20g), grated
1 tablespoon finely chopped
  fresh lemon grass
3 fresh small red thai chillies,
  chopped finely
⅓ cup (80ml) sweet sherry
2 teaspoons cornflour
½ cup (125ml) water
2 tablespoons mirin
1 tablespoon soy sauce
12 green onions, sliced thinly
¼ cup coarsely chopped
  fresh mint
¼ cup coarsely chopped
  fresh coriander

1 Scrub mussels under cold water;
   discard beards.
2 Cook rice in medium saucepan
   of boiling water, uncovered, until
   just tender. Drain; cover to
   keep warm.
3 Meanwhile, heat oil in wok or
   large frying pan; stir-fry ginger,
   lemon grass and chilli until
   fragrant. Add mussels and
   sherry; cook, covered, about
   5 minutes or until mussels open
   (discard any that do not).
4 Blend cornflour with the water,
   mirin and soy sauce in small jug;
   add to wok, stir-fry until mixture
   boils and thickens slightly. Remove
   from heat; stir in onion and herbs.
   Serve mussels with rice.

serves 4
per serving 6.4g fat;
1550kJ (370 cal)

artichoke hearts in white-wine vinaigrette

PREPARATION TIME 45 MINUTES **COOKING TIME** 30 MINUTES (PLUS STANDING TIME)

1 lemon, chopped coarsely
20 small globe artichokes (2kg)
2 cups (500ml) dry white wine
¼ cup loosely packed fresh
   thyme leaves
5 cloves garlic, unpeeled
½ cup (125ml) lemon juice
2 teaspoons sea salt flakes
1 cup (250ml) white
   wine vinegar
2 cups (500ml) water
1 tablespoon extra virgin
   olive oil

1 Cut piece of baking paper into a circle to fit inside large saucepan. Place lemon in large bowl half-filled with cold water.

2 Discard outer leaves from artichokes; cut tips from remaining leaves. Trim then peel stalks; place artichokes in lemon water.

3 Combine wine, thyme, garlic, juice, salt, vinegar, the 2 cups of water and drained artichokes in large saucepan, cover with baking paper round; bring to a boil. Reduce heat; simmer, covered, about 25 minutes or until artichokes are just tender. Cool in poaching liquid 30 minutes. Whisk ½ cup of the poaching liquid in small bowl with oil (discard remaining liquid).

4 Halve artichokes vertically; using small knife, remove chokes. Divide artichokes among serving bowls; drizzle with poaching liquid mixture.

serves 4
per serving 5.5g fat;
912kJ (218 cal)

mulled-wine pork and stone fruits

PREPARATION TIME 15 MINUTES **COOKING TIME** 15 MINUTES

"Mulled" wine has been heated and spiced, and is a favourite winter drink in cold climates. Here, we've used the best of the summer's stone-fruit crop to prove that mulled wine can be consumed any time of year!

2 cups (500ml) water
1 cup (250ml) dry white wine
½ cup (110g) sugar
2 cinnamon sticks
5 cloves
¼ cup (60ml) brandy
2 medium peaches (300g), stoned, quartered
4 medium plums (450g), stoned, quartered
2 medium nectarines (340g), stoned, quartered
4 medium apricots (200g), stoned, quartered
800g pork fillets, trimmed
1 fresh long red chilli, sliced thinly
1 long green chilli, sliced thinly

1 Combine the water, wine and sugar in heated large frying pan, stirring constantly, without boiling, until sugar dissolves; bring to a boil. Add cinnamon, cloves, brandy and fruit, reduce heat; simmer, uncovered, about 5 minutes or until fruit is just tender. Using slotted spoon, transfer fruit to large bowl; cover to keep warm.

2 Return poaching liquid to a boil; add pork. Reduce heat; simmer, covered, about 10 minutes or until pork is cooked as desired. Cool pork in liquid 10 minutes then slice thickly. Discard poaching liquid.

3 Combine chillies with fruit; divide fruit and any fruit juices among serving bowls, top with pork.

serves 4
per serving 4.9g fat; 2023kJ (483 cal)

desserts

mango lime syrup cake

PREPARATION TIME 20 MINUTES **COOKING TIME** 20 MINUTES

10g butter, melted

2 tablespoons brown sugar

1 large mango (600g),
   sliced thinly

2 eggs

⅓ cup (75g) caster sugar

½ cup (75g) wheaten cornflour

1 tablespoon custard powder

½ teaspoon cream of tartar

¼ teaspoon bicarbonate
   of soda

LIME SYRUP

⅓ cup (80ml) water

¾ cup (165g) caster sugar

⅓ cup (80ml) lime juice

2 teaspoons finely grated
   lime rind

1 Preheat oven to moderately hot. Lightly grease deep 22cm-round cake pan.

2 Pour butter over base of prepared pan; sift brown sugar evenly over butter, top with mango slices.

3 Beat eggs and sugar in small bowl with electric mixer about 5 minutes or until thick and creamy.

4 Sift dry ingredients three times onto baking paper; fold into egg mixture. Pour sponge mixture into pan; bake, uncovered, in moderately hot oven about 20 minutes.

5 Meanwhile, make lime syrup.

6 Turn cake onto wire rack set over tray; pour half of the lime syrup over hot cake. Serve remaining syrup with cake.

LIME SYRUP Stir the water, sugar and juice in small saucepan over heat, without boiling, until sugar dissolves; bring to a boil. Boil, uncovered, without stirring, about 5 minutes or until syrup thickens slightly. Cool 10 minutes; stir in rind.

serves 8
per serving 2.7g fat; 944kJ (226 cal)

TIP You can make lime syrup a day ahead; refrigerate covered.

lemon sorbet

PREPARATION TIME 15 MINUTES (PLUS STANDING AND FREEZING TIME) **COOKING TIME** 10 MINUTES

You need four lemons for
this recipe.

2½ cups (625ml) water
¼ cup finely grated lemon rind
1 cup (220g) caster sugar
¾ cup (180ml) lemon juice
1 egg white

1 Stir the water, rind and sugar
   in small saucepan over heat,
   without boiling, until sugar
   dissolves; bring to a boil. Boil,
   uncovered, without stirring, about
   5 minutes or until syrup thickens
   slightly. Strain into medium
   heatproof jug; cool to room
   temperature. Stir in juice.
2 Pour sorbet mixture into
   14cm x 21cm loaf pan, cover
   with foil; freeze about 3 hours
   or until almost set.
3 Blend or process mixture with
   egg white until smooth. Return
   to pan, cover; freeze 3 hours
   or overnight.

serves 4
per serving 0.1g fat;
957kJ (229 cal)

TIP You can also freeze the
sorbet-egg white mixture in an
ice-cream machine following the
manufacturer's instructions.

watermelon sorbet

PREPARATION TIME 15 MINUTES (PLUS STANDING AND FREEZING TIME) **COOKING TIME** 10 MINUTES

You need a 1.2kg piece of watermelon for this recipe.

½ cup (125ml) water
½ cup (110g) caster sugar
850g coarsely chopped
    seedless watermelon
1 egg white

1 Stir the water and sugar in small saucepan over heat, without boiling, until sugar dissolves; bring to a boil. Boil, uncovered, without stirring, about 5 minutes or until syrup thickens slightly. Transfer to large heatproof jug; cool to room temperature.

2 Meanwhile, blend or process watermelon until smooth; strain through fine sieve into cooled sugar syrup. Stir to combine.

3 Pour sorbet mixture into 14cm x 21cm loaf pan, cover with foil; freeze about 3 hours or until almost set.

4 Blend or process mixture with egg white until smooth. Return to pan, cover; freeze 3 hours or overnight.

serves 4
per serving 1.5g fat;
660kJ (158 cal)

TIP You can also freeze the sorbet-egg white mixture in an ice-cream machine following the manufacturer's instructions.

blueberry and fillo pastry stacks

PREPARATION TIME 15 MINUTES **COOKING TIME** 10 MINUTES

4 sheets fillo pastry
cooking-oil spray
125g packaged light cream cheese
½ cup (125ml) light cream
2 teaspoons finely grated orange rind
2 tablespoons icing sugar mixture

BLUEBERRY SAUCE

300g blueberries
¼ cup (55g) caster sugar
2 tablespoons orange juice
1 teaspoon cornflour

1   Preheat oven to moderately hot. Lightly grease oven trays.
2   Spray one fillo sheet with oil; layer with another fillo sheet. Halve fillo
    stack lengthways; cut each half into thirds to form six fillo squares.
    Repeat process with remaining fillo sheets. Place 12 fillo squares
    onto prepared trays; spray with oil. Bake, uncovered, in moderately
    hot oven about 5 minutes or until browned lightly; cool 10 minutes.
3   Meanwhile, make blueberry sauce.
4   Beat cheese, cream, rind and half of the sugar in small bowl with
    electric mixer until smooth.
5   Place one fillo square on each serving plate; spoon half of the cheese
    mixture and half of the blueberry sauce over squares. Repeat layering
    process, finishing with fillo squares; dust with remaining sifted sugar.
    BLUEBERRY SAUCE Cook blueberries, sugar and half of the juice in
    small saucepan, stirring, until sugar dissolves. Stir in blended cornflour
    and remaining juice; cook, stirring, until mixture boils and thickens slightly.
    Remove from heat; cool 10 minutes.

serves 4
per serving 13g fat; 1267kJ (302 cal)

stone-fruit jelly

PREPARATION TIME 15 MINUTES (PLUS REFRIGERATION TIME) **COOKING TIME** 10 MINUTES

We used a sparkling white wine having a sweet, fruity flavour for this recipe.

½ cup (110g) caster sugar
3 cups (750ml) sparkling
    white wine
2 tablespoons gelatine
½ cup (125ml) water
2 tablespoons lemon juice
1 large nectarine (170g),
    sliced thinly
2 medium apricots (100g),
    sliced thinly
1 medium peach (150g),
    sliced thinly
150g raspberries

1   Combine sugar and 1 cup of the wine in small saucepan; bring to a boil. Reduce heat; simmer, uncovered, 5 minutes. Transfer to large heatproof bowl.
2   Meanwhile, sprinkle gelatine over the water in small heatproof jug; stand jug in small saucepan of simmering water. Stir until gelatine dissolves.
3   Whisk gelatine mixture and juice into warm wine mixture. Stir in remaining wine.
4   Divide fruit among four 1¼-cup (310ml) serving glasses; pour wine mixture over fruit. Cover; refrigerate about 3 hours or until set.

serves 4
per serving 0.3g fat;
1274kJ (304 cal)

crushed pavlovas with honey yogurt and mixed berries

PREPARATION TIME 15 MINUTES

Use any combination of your favourite berries in this recipe; if fresh ones are unavailable, you can use thawed frozen berries.

250g strawberries, halved
150g blueberries
120g raspberries
10 mini pavlova shells (100g)
1kg honey yogurt

1 Combine berries in medium bowl. Crush pavlovas coarsely into small bowl.
2 Divide yogurt among serving bowls; sprinkle with berries and crushed pavlova.

serves 6
per serving 5.1g fat;
1046kJ (250 cal)

TIPS This recipe should be made just before serving. We used mini pavlova shells here, but a single large pavlova shell can be used instead.

cheese-filled crepe triangles with caramelised oranges

PREPARATION TIME 25 MINUTES (PLUS REFRIGERATION TIME) **COOKING TIME** 30 MINUTES

You need one lemon, four passionfruit and about six small oranges for this recipe.

1½ cups (300g) ricotta cheese
2 teaspoons caster sugar
2 teaspoons lemon juice
¼ teaspoon ground cinnamon
¾ cup (110g) plain flour
1 tablespoon caster sugar, extra
1 egg
1⅓ cups (330ml) no-fat milk
1 teaspoon vegetable oil
1 tablespoon coarsely chopped
    fresh mint

CARAMELISED ORANGES

1kg small oranges
¼ cup (60ml) water
½ cup (55g) caster sugar
⅓ cup (80ml) passionfruit pulp
1 tablespoon lemon juice

1 Place cheese in muslin-lined strainer or colander set over large bowl. Cover then weight cheese with an upright saucer topped with a heavy can. Drain overnight in refrigerator; discard liquid.

2 Mix drained cheese in medium bowl with sugar, juice and cinnamon, cover; refrigerate until required.

3 Combine flour and extra sugar in medium bowl; gradually whisk in combined egg, milk and oil until batter is smooth. Strain into large jug, cover; refrigerate 30 minutes.

4 Meanwhile, make caramelised oranges.

5 Pour 2 tablespoons of the batter into heated lightly greased 18cm non-stick frying pan; cook crepe until browned lightly both sides. Repeat process with remaining batter; you will have 12 crepes.

6 Spoon equal amounts of the cheese mixture onto a quarter section of each crepe; fold crepe in half over filling and then in half again to enclose filling and form triangular parcels. Divide filled crepes among serving plates; top with equal amounts of caramelised oranges and mint.
CARAMELISED ORANGES Remove peel and pith from oranges over small bowl to save juice; slice oranges thinly. Stir the water and sugar in medium saucepan, without boiling, until sugar dissolves; bring to a boil. Boil, uncovered, without stirring, about 5 minutes or until mixture begins to brown. Add passionfruit, lemon juice and reserved orange juice; cook, stirring occasionally, until any pieces of toffee dissolve. Cool 10 minutes; stir in orange slices.

serves 4
per serving 11.6g fat; 1723kJ (411 cal)

tropical fruit skewers with coconut dressing

PREPARATION TIME 30 MINUTES **COOKING TIME** 5 MINUTES

You need eight long bamboo skewers for this recipe.

2 medium bananas (400g)
½ medium pineapple (625g)
2 large starfruit (320g)
1 large mango (600g),
    chopped coarsely

COCONUT DRESSING
⅓ cup (80ml) coconut-
    flavoured liqueur
¼ cup (60ml) light coconut milk
1 tablespoon grated
    palm sugar
1cm piece fresh ginger
    (5g), grated

1 Make coconut dressing.
2 Cut each unpeeled banana
    into eight pieces. Cut unpeeled
    pineapple into eight slices; cut
    slices in half. Cut each starfruit
    into eight slices.
3 Thread fruit onto skewers,
    alternating varieties. Cook
    skewers on grill plate (or grill or
    barbecue), brushing with a little
    of the dressing, until browned
    lightly. Serve skewers drizzled
    with remaining dressing.
COCONUT DRESSING
Place ingredients in screw-top
jar; shake well.

serves 4
per serving 1.3g fat;
1041kJ (249 cal)

TIP We used Malibu for the
dressing, but you can use any
coconut-flavoured liqueur.

apricot and honey soufflés

PREPARATION TIME 15 MINUTES **COOKING TIME** 30 MINUTES

¼ cup (55g) caster sugar
4 apricots (200g)
¼ cup (60ml) water
2 tablespoons honey
4 egg whites

1 Preheat oven to moderately hot. Lightly grease six ¾-cup (180ml) ovenproof dishes; sprinkle insides of dishes with a little of the sugar, place on oven tray.

2 Place apricots in small heatproof bowl, cover with boiling water; stand 2 minutes. Drain; cool 5 minutes. Peel and seed apricots; chop flesh finely.

3 Combine apricot in small saucepan with the water, honey and remaining sugar; bring to a boil. Reduce heat; simmer, uncovered, about 10 minutes or until apricots soften to a jam-like consistency.

4 Beat egg whites in small bowl with electric mixer until soft peaks form. With motor operating, gradually add hot apricot mixture, beating until combined. Spoon soufflé mixture into prepared dishes; bake, uncovered, in moderately hot oven about 15 minutes or until soufflés are browned lightly.

serves 6
per serving 0.1g fat;
357kJ (85 cal)

tropical fruit salad

PREPARATION TIME 20 MINUTES (PLUS STANDING AND REFRIGERATION TIME) **COOKING TIME** 15 MINUTES

You need three passionfruit for this recipe.

2 cups (500ml) water
⅓ cup (135g) grated palm sugar
2cm piece fresh ginger (10g), chopped finely
2 star anise
2 tablespoons lime juice
¼ cup coarsely chopped fresh mint
2 large mangoes (1.2kg), diced into 2cm pieces
1 small honeydew melon (900g), diced into 2cm pieces
1 small pineapple (800g), chopped coarsely
2 medium oranges (480g), segmented
¼ cup (60ml) passionfruit pulp
12 fresh lychees (300g), halved

1 Stir the water and sugar in small saucepan over heat, without boiling, until sugar dissolves; bring to a boil. Boil, uncovered, without stirring, 5 minutes. Add ginger and star anise; simmer, uncovered, about 5 minutes or until syrup thickens slightly. Discard star anise; cool to room temperature. Stir in juice and mint.
2 Place prepared fruit in large bowl with syrup; toss gently to combine. Refrigerate until cold.

serves 6
per serving 0.8g fat;
1181kJ (282 cal)

ginger and almond biscotti ice-cream sandwiches

PREPARATION TIME 25 MINUTES (PLUS STANDING AND REFRIGERATION TIME) **COOKING TIME** 45 MINUTES

3 egg whites
½ cup (110g) caster sugar
1 teaspoon vanilla extract
¾ cup (110g) plain flour
¼ cup (30g) almond meal
2 tablespoons finely chopped
   crystallised ginger
¼ cup (40g) toasted
   blanched almonds
⅔ cup (160ml) low-fat
   ice-cream

1 Preheat oven to moderate. Lightly grease 8cm x 25cm bar cake pan; line base and long sides with baking paper, extending paper 5cm over sides of pan.
2 Beat egg whites in small bowl with electric mixer until soft peaks form. With motor operating, gradually add sugar, beating, until sugar dissolves. Beat in extract then fold in flour, almond meal, ginger and nuts.
3 Spread mixture into prepared pan; bake, uncovered, in moderate oven about 25 minutes or until firm. Cool to room temperature in pan. Cover; refrigerate 2 hours.
4 Preheat oven to moderately slow. Line oven tray with baking paper. Trim short ends of loaf; cut loaf crossways into four equal pieces. Trim all brown sides from pieces; slice each piece horizontally into four pieces.
5 Place pieces on prepared tray; bake, uncovered, in moderately slow oven about 20 minutes or until biscotti are crisp and browned lightly. Cool on tray. Sandwich biscotti with ice-cream.

makes 8
per sandwich 5g fat; 729kJ (174 cal)

TIP Biscotti can be made up to a week ahead and kept in an airtight container.

balsamic strawberries with black pepper wafers

PREPARATION TIME 15 MINUTES (PLUS STANDING AND REFRIGERATION TIME) **COOKING TIME** 5 MINUTES

750g strawberries, halved
¼ cup (55g) caster sugar
2 tablespoons balsamic vinegar
¼ cup (35g) plain flour
2 tablespoons caster
   sugar, extra
1 egg white
30g butter, melted
½ teaspoon vanilla extract
½ teaspoon freshly ground
   black pepper

1 Preheat oven to moderate. Line oven tray with baking paper.
2 Combine strawberries, sugar and vinegar in medium bowl, cover; refrigerate 1 hour.
3 Meanwhile, using wooden spoon, beat flour, extra sugar, egg white, butter and extract in small bowl until smooth.
4 Place one level teaspoon of the wafer mixture on prepared tray; using back of spoon, spread mixture into 8cm circle. Repeat with remaining wafer mixture, allowing 2cm between each wafer. Sprinkle each wafer with black pepper; bake, uncovered, in moderate oven about 5 minutes or until browned lightly. Cool 15 minutes. Serve strawberry mixture with wafers.

serves 4
per serving 6.4g fat;
808kJ (193 cal)

coffee granita with walnut crisps

PREPARATION TIME 25 MINUTES (PLUS FREEZING TIME) **COOKING TIME** 10 MINUTES

2 cups (500ml) boiling water
¼ cup (30g) ground
    coffee beans
⅓ cup (75g) caster sugar
10g butter
1 tablespoon honey
1 tablespoon plain flour
1 tablespoon icing
    sugar mixture
2 tablespoons finely chopped
    roasted walnuts

1 Pour the water over coffee in small plunger; stand 5 minutes before plunging and pouring into medium jug. Add caster sugar; stir until sugar dissolves. Pour coffee into 20cm x 30cm lamington pan, cover with foil; freeze about 3 hours or until almost set.

2 Using fork, scrape granita from bottom and sides of pan, mixing frozen with unfrozen mixture, cover; return to freezer. Repeat process every hour for about 4 hours or until large ice crystals form and granita has a dry, shard-like appearance.

3 Meanwhile, melt butter with honey in small saucepan over low heat; stir in flour, icing sugar and nuts. Place walnut crisp mixture into small bowl, cover; refrigerate 1 hour.

4 Preheat oven to hot. Line oven trays with baking paper.

5 Drop level teaspoons of the crisp mixture on prepared trays about 10cm apart; bake, uncovered, in hot oven about 3 minutes or until crisps are browned lightly. Remove from oven; cool 1 minute. Using spatula, lift crisps carefully and place over rolling pin to cool. Serve granita with walnut crisps.

serves 4
per serving 4.9g fat; 696kJ (166 cal)

vanilla panna cotta with berry compote

PREPARATION TIME 15 MINUTES (PLUS REFRIGERATION TIME) **COOKING TIME** 10 MINUTES

2 tablespoons boiling water
2 tablespoons honey
1 vanilla bean
2 teaspoons gelatine
1½ cups (380g) yogurt

BERRY COMPOTE
2 cups (300g) frozen mixed berries
¼ cup (40g) icing sugar mixture

1 Combine the water and honey in small heatproof jug. Split vanilla
   bean in half lengthways; scrape seeds into jug then place pod
   in jug. Sprinkle gelatine over honey mixture; stand jug in small
   saucepan of simmering water. Stir until gelatine dissolves; cool
   5 minutes. Discard vanilla pod.
2 Combine honey mixture and yogurt in small bowl; stir until smooth.
   Strain into four ½-cup (125ml) moulds, cover; refrigerate 3 hours
   or overnight.
3 Meanwhile, make berry compote.
4 Turn panna cotta onto serving plates; serve with berry compote.
   BERRY COMPOTE Combine berries and sugar in medium
   saucepan over low heat, uncovered, stirring occasionally, about
   5 minutes or until berries just soften. Transfer to small bowl;
   cool 10 minutes. Cover; refrigerate until required.

serves 4
per serving 1.9g fat; 768kJ (183 cal)

TIP Wipe the outsides of panna cotta moulds with a hot cloth
to make turning them onto plates easier.

glossary

acidulated water water to which lemon juice or pulp has been added to prevent the cut surfaces of foods, such as artichokes and apples, from discolouring.

almonds

BLANCHED whole nuts with brown skins removed.

MEAL also known as finely ground almonds; powdered to a flour-like texture, and used in baking or as a thickening agent.

basil an aromatic herb; there are many types, but the most commonly used is sweet basil.

THAI also known as horapa; different from sweet basil in both look and taste. Having smaller leaves and purplish stems, it has a slight licorice or aniseed taste, and is one of the basic flavours that typify thai cuisine.

bean sprouts also known as bean shoots; tender new growths of assorted beans and seeds germinated for consumption in salads and stir-fries. The most readily available are mung bean, soy bean, alfalfa and snow pea sprouts. Sprout mixtures or salads are also available, if you prefer.

beetroot also known as red beets or just beets; firm, round root vegetable. Can be eaten raw (grated in salads), boiled (sliced), roasted (whole) or mashed (like potatoes).

bicarbonate of soda also known as baking or carb soda.

black beans also known as turtle beans; Cuban or Latin American rather than Chinese in origin. Jet black with a tiny white eye, black beans can be found in most greengrocers and delicatessens.

bok choy also known as bak choy, pak choy and chinese white cabbage; has a mild mustard taste. Use both stems and leaves, stir-fried, braised and raw in salads. Baby bok choy is also available, it is smaller and slightly more tender, and is often cooked whole.

breadcrumbs

PACKAGED fine-textured, crunchy, purchased, white breadcrumbs.

STALE one- or two-day-old bread made into crumbs by grating, blending or processing.

butter use salted or unsalted (sweet) butter; 125g is equal to one stick of butter.

capers the grey-green buds of a warm climate (usually Mediterranean) shrub, sold either dried and salted, or pickled in a vinegar brine; tiny young ones, called baby capers, are also available.

capsicum also known as pepper or bell pepper. Native to Central and South America, they can be red, green, yellow, orange or purplish-black. Discard seeds and membranes before use.

cardamom native to India and used extensively in its cuisine; can be purchased in pod, seed or ground form. Has a distinctive, aromatic, sweetly rich flavour; one of the world's most expensive spices.

cheese

COTTAGE fresh, white, unripened curd cheese with a grainy consistency and a fat content between 5% and 15%.

FETTA salty white cheese, is one of the cornerstones of the Greek kitchen. Most commonly made from cow milk, though sheep and goat varieties are available.

HALOUMI a cream-coloured sheep-milk cheese matured in brine; somewhat like a minty, salty fetta in flavour. Haloumi can be grilled or fried, briefly, without breaking down.

PARMESAN also known as parmigiano, parmesan is a hard, grainy cow-milk cheese that originated in the Parma region of Italy. The curd is salted in brine for a month before being aged for up to two years in humid conditions. Parmesan is mainly grated as a topping for pasta, soups and other savoury dishes, but is also delicious eaten with fruit.

RICOTTA a low-fat, fresh unripened cheese made from whey; we used a variety with a fat content of not more than 8.5%.

char siu sauce a chinese barbecue sauce made from sugar, water, salt, fermented soy bean paste, honey, soy sauce, malt syrup and spices. It can be found at most supermarkets.

chickpeas also called garbanzos, hummus or channa; an irregularly round, sandy-coloured legume used extensively in mediterranean and latin cooking.

chilli generally the smaller the chilli, the hotter it is. Use rubber gloves when seeding and chopping fresh chillies as they can burn your skin. Removing seeds and membranes lessens the heat level.

FLAKES deep-red, dehydrated chilli slices and whole seeds; good for use in cooking or as a condiment for sprinkling over cooked foods.

THAI bright red to dark green in colour, ranging in size from small ("scuds") to long and thin; among the hottest of chillies.

chinese cabbage also known as peking cabbage or wong bok.

cloves dried flower buds of a tropical tree; can be used whole or in ground form. Has a strong scent and taste so should be used minimally.

coriander also known as cilantro or chinese parsley; bright-green leafy herb with a pungent flavour. Often stirred into or sprinkled over a dish just before serving for maximum impact. Both the stems and roots of coriander are also used in thai cooking; wash well before chopping.

cornflour also known as cornstarch; used as a thickening agent in cooking.

WHEATEN seemingly contradictory because this variation is made from the fine starch extracted from wheat, not corn (maize).

cornichon a very small variety of cucumber. Pickled, they are traditionally served with pâté; the Swiss always serve them with fondue or raclette, a melting cheese.

couscous a fine, grain-like cereal product, originally from North Africa; made from semolina.

cucumber, lebanese short, thin-skinned and slender; this variety is also known as the european or burpless cucumber.

daikon giant radish with sweet, fresh flavour. The daikon's flesh is crisp, juicy and white, while the skin can be either creamy white or black. It can range from 15cm to 40cm in length with an average diameter of 5cm to 7cm. Choose those that are firm and unwrinkled. Refrigerate, wrapped in a plastic bag, up to a week.

eggplant purple-skinned vegetable also known as aubergine.

five-spice powder a fragrant mixture of ground cinnamon, cloves, star anise, sichuan pepper and fennel seeds.

flour

PLAIN an all-purpose flour, made from wheat.

gai larn also known as kanah, gai lum, chinese broccoli and chinese kale; appreciated more for its stems than its coarse leaves. Can be served, steamed and stir-fried, in soups and noodle dishes.

ginger also known as green or root ginger; the thick gnarled root of a tropical plant. Can be kept, peeled and covered with dry sherry, in a jar, and refrigerated or frozen.

PICKLED PINK available, packaged, from Asian grocery stores; pickled paper-thin shavings of ginger in a mixture of vinegar, sugar and natural colouring.

CRYSTALLISED fresh ginger cubed and preserved in syrup then coated in sugar.

globe artichokes large flower-bud of a member of the thistle family. Has tough petal-like leaves; edible in part when cooked.

gow gee wrappers wonton wrappers, spring roll or egg pastry sheets can be substituted.

green peppercorns soft, unripe berry of the pepper plant, usually sold packed in brine (occasionally found dried, packed in salt). Has a distinctive fresh taste that goes well with mustard or cream sauces.

kaffir lime leaves also known as bai magrood; used like bay leaves or curry leaves, especially in thai cooking. Are aromatic leaves of a small citrus tree bearing a wrinkled-skinned yellow-green fruit; originally grown in South Africa and South-East Asia. Looks like two glossy, dark green leaves joined end to end, forming an hourglass shape. Sold fresh, dried or frozen.

kalonji also known as nigella or black onion seeds; teardrop-shaped seeds used extensively in indian cooking to impart a sharp, almost nutty flavour.

kecap manis sweet, thick soy sauce that has sugar and spices added.

kipfler potatoes small, finger-shaped potato having a nutty flavour.

kumara Polynesian name of orange-fleshed sweet potato often confused with yam.

lamb backstrap the larger fillet from a row of loin chops or cutlets.

lamington pan 20cm x 30cm slab cake pan, 3cm deep.

lemon grass a tall, clumping, lemon-smelling and -tasting, sharp-edged grass; the white lower part of each stem is chopped and used in asian cooking or for tea.

lentils (red, brown, yellow) dried pulses often identified by and named after their colour; also known as dhal.

PUY originally from the region of the same name in France; small, dark-green, fast-cooking lentils with a delicate flavour.

light sour cream we used a low-fat sour cream having a fat content of 18.5%.

Malibu a coconut-flavoured rum liqueur.

mince meat also known as ground meat, as in beef, pork, lamb and chicken.

mirin champagne-coloured japanese cooking wine made of glutinous rice and alcohol; used expressly for cooking and should not be confused with sake. Also available is a seasoned sweet mirin called manjo mirin that is made of water, rice, corn syrup and alcohol.

mushrooms

BUTTON small, cultivated white mushrooms having a delicate, subtle flavour.

FLAT large, flat mushrooms with a rich earthy flavour; ideal for barbecuing and filling. They are sometimes misnamed field mushrooms, which are wild mushrooms.

SHIITAKE when fresh are also known as forest, golden oak or chinese black mushrooms; although cultivated, have the earthiness and taste of wild mushrooms. Are large and meaty; often used as a substitute for meat in some asian vegetarian dishes. When dried, are known as donko or dried chinese mushrooms; rehydrate before use.

SWISS BROWN also known as cremini or roman mushrooms, are light brown mushrooms with a full-bodied flavour. Button or cup mushrooms can be substituted.

no-fat milk we used

milk with 0.15% fat content or lower.

noodles

BEAN THREAD also known as wun sen, made from extruded mung bean paste; also known as cellophane or glass noodles because they are transparent when cooked. White in colour (not off-white like rice vermicelli), very delicate and fine; available dried in various-sized bundles. Must be soaked to soften before use; using them deep-fried requires no pre-soaking.

FRESH EGG also known as yellow noodles; made from wheat flour and eggs, sold fresh and dried. Range in size from very fine strands to wide, thick spaghetti-like pieces as thick as a shoelace.

PAPPARDELLE also sometimes called lasagnette or mafalde; flat, wide pasta ribbons sometimes having scalloped edges. Tagliatelle, fettuccine or narrow lasagne can be substituted.

RICE STICK a dried noodle, available flat and wide or very thin; made from rice flour and water. Especially popular in south-east asian cooking. Should be soaked in hot water until soft.

SOBA thin spaghetti-like pale brown noodle made from varying amounts of buckwheat and plain flour; used in soups and stir-fries or eaten cold.

oil

COOKING-OIL SPRAY we used a cholesterol-free cooking spray made from canola oil.

OLIVE made from ripened olives. Extra virgin and virgin are the best, while extra light or light refers to taste not fat levels.

PEANUT pressed from ground peanuts; most commonly used oil in asian cooking because of its high smoke point (capacity to handle high heat without burning).

SESAME made from roasted, crushed, white sesame seeds; a flavouring rather than a cooking medium.

VEGETABLE any of a number of oils sourced from plants rather than animal fats.

onion

BROWN AND WHITE are interchangeable. Their pungent flesh adds flavour to a vast range of dishes.

GREEN also known as scallion or, incorrectly, shallot; an immature onion picked before the bulb has formed, having a long, bright-green edible stalk.

RED also known as spanish, red spanish or bermuda onion; a sweet-flavoured, large, purple-red onion that is particularly good eaten in raw salads.

paprika ground, dried red capsicum (bell pepper), available sweet or hot.

parsley, flat-leaf also known as continental parsley or italian parsley.

passionfruit also known as granadilla; a small tropical fruit, native to Brazil, comprised of a tough outer skin surrounding edible black sweet-sour seeds.

pearl barley a nutritious grain used in soups and stews as well as in whisky- and beer-making. Pearl barley has had the husk discarded and been hulled and polished, much the same as rice.

pepitas dried pumpkin seeds; available from most supermarkets and health food stores.

pide also known as turkish bread, comes in long (about 45cm) flat loaves as well as individual rounds; made from wheat flour and sprinkled with sesame seeds or kalonji.

pine nuts also known as pignoli; not, in fact, a nut but a small, cream-coloured kernel from pine cones.

pitta also called lebanese bread; a wheat-flour pocket bread sold in large, flat pieces that separate easily into two thin rounds. Also available in small thick pieces called pocket pitta.

polenta a flour-like cereal made of ground corn (maize); fine-textured cornmeal. Also the name of the dish made from it.

preserved lemon rind a North African specialty; lemons are quartered and preserved in salt and lemon juice. To use, discard pulp, squeeze juice from rind, rinse rind well; slice thinly. Serve as part of a mezze or use in casseroles or tagines to add flavour. Sold in jars or singly by delicatessens; store, under refrigeration, once opened.

radicchio burgundy-leaved lettuce with white ribs and slightly bitter flavour.

rice

BROWN natural whole grain.

JASMINE fragrant white long-grained rice; white rice can be substituted, but will not taste the same.

risoni small, rice-shaped pasta similar to orzo; good used in soups and salads.

rocket also known as arugula, rugula and rucola; a peppery-tasting green leaf that can be used similarly to baby spinach leaves, eaten raw in salad or used in cooking. Baby rocket leaves are both smaller and less peppery.

saffron stigma of a member of the crocus family, available in strands or ground form; imparts a yellow-orange colour to food once infused. Quality varies greatly; the best is the most expensive spice in the world. Should be stored in the freezer.

sambal oelek (also ulek or olek) Indonesian in origin; a salty paste made from ground chillies and vinegar.

sauces

FISH also called nam pla or nuoc nam; made from pulverised salted fermented fish, most often anchovies. Has a pungent smell and strong taste; use sparingly.

HOISIN a thick, sweet and spicy chinese paste made from salted fermented soy beans, onions and garlic; used as a marinade or baste, or to accent stir-fries and barbecued or roasted foods.

OYSTER Asian in origin, this rich, brown sauce is made from oysters and their brine, cooked with salt and soy sauce, and thickened with starches.

SOY also known as sieu; made from fermented soy beans. Several variations are available in most supermarkets and Asian food stores.

SWEET CHILLI a comparatively mild, thai sauce made from red chillies, sugar, garlic and vinegar.

TABASCO brand name of an extremely fiery sauce made from vinegar, hot red peppers and salt.

WORCESTERSHIRE a thin, dark-brown spicy sauce used as a seasoning for meat, gravies and cocktails and as a condiment.

sesame seeds black and white are the most common varieties of this small oval seed, however there are also red and brown varieties. A good source of calcium; used in cuisines the world over as an ingredient in cooking and as a condiment. To toast: spread seeds evenly on oven tray, toast in moderate oven briefly.

sherry fortified wine consumed as an aperitif or used in cooking. Sold as fino (dry, light), amontillado (medium sweet, dark) and oloroso (full-bodied, very dark).

spinach also known as english spinach and, incorrectly, silverbeet. Tender green leaves are good uncooked in salads or added to soups, stir-fries and stews.

starfruit also known as carambola, five-corner fruit or chinese star fruit; pale green or yellow colour. Has a clean, crisp texture; flavour may be either sweet or sour, depending on variety and when picked. Don't need to be peeled or seeded. Are slow to discolour; avoid ones with brown spots or streaks.

star anise a dried star-shaped pod having an astringent aniseed flavour; used to favour stocks and marinades.

stock available in cans, bottles or tetra packs. Stock cubes, powder or concentrated liquid can be used. As a guide, 1 teaspoon of stock powder or 1 small crumbled stock cube or 1 portion stock concentrate mixed with 1 cup (250ml) water will give a fairly strong stock. Be aware of the salt and fat content of stocks.

sugar we used coarse granulated table sugar, also known as crystal sugar, unless otherwise specified.

BROWN a soft, fine sugar retaining molasses for its colour and flavour.

CASTER also known as superfine or finely granulated table sugar.

ICING SUGAR MIXTURE also known as confectioners' sugar or powdered sugar; granulated sugar crushed together with a small amount (about 3%) cornflour added.

PALM also known as nam tan pip, jaggery, and jawa or gula melaka; made from the sap of the sugar palm tree. Light-brown to black in colour and usually sold in rock-hard cakes; substitute brown sugar if unavailable.

sugar snap peas also known as honey snap peas; fresh small pea that can be eaten whole, pod and all, similarly to snow peas.

sumac a purple-red, astringent spice ground from berries growing on shrubs that flourish wild around the Mediterranean; adds a tart, lemony flavour to dips and dressings and goes well with barbecued meat. Can be found in Middle-Eastern food stores. Substitute: ½ teaspoon lemon pepper + 1/8 teaspoon allspice + 1/8 teaspoon five spice = ¾ teaspoon sumac.

taco seasoning mix a packaged seasoning meant to duplicate the mexican sauce made from spices including oregano, cumin, and chillies.

vanilla bean dried long, thin pod from a tropical golden orchid grown in Tahiti and Central and South America; the minuscule black seeds inside the bean are used to impart a luscious vanilla flavour in baking and desserts.

vietnamese mint not a mint at all, this pungent, narrow-leafed herb, also known as cambodian mint and laksa leaf (daun laksa), is widely used in many asian soups and salads.

vinegar

BALSAMIC authentic only from the province of Modena, Italy; made from a regional wine of white Trebbiano grapes specially processed then aged in antique wooden casks to give the exquisite pungent flavour.

RASPBERRY made from fresh raspberries steeped in a white wine vinegar.

RED WINE based on fermented red wine.

RICE a colourless vinegar made from fermented rice and flavoured with sugar and salt. Also known as seasoned rice vinegar.

WHITE WINE made from white wine.

wasabi asian horseradish used to make the pungent, green-coloured condiment traditionally served with japanese raw-fish dishes; sold in powdered or paste form. Available from Asian food stores.

wonton wrappers also known as wonton skins; made of flour, eggs and water. Sold packaged in large amounts and found in the refrigerated section of Asian grocery stores; gow gee, egg or spring roll pastry sheets can be substituted.

yaki-nori a type of dried seaweed used in japanese cooking as a flavouring, garnish or for sushi. Sold in thin sheets.

zucchini also known as courgette; small green, yellow or white vegetable belonging to the squash family.

index

facts and figures

Wherever you live, you'll be able to use our recipes with the help of these easy-to-follow conversions. While these conversions are approximate only, the difference between an exact and the approximate conversion of various liquid and dry measures is but minimal, and will not affect your cooking results.

dry measures

metric	imperial
15g	½oz
30g	1oz
60g	2oz
90g	3oz
125g	4oz (¼lb)
155g	5oz
185g	6oz
220g	7oz
250g	8oz (½lb)
280g	9oz
315g	10oz
345g	11oz
375g	12oz (¾lb)
410g	13oz
440g	14oz
470g	15oz
500g	16oz (1lb)
750g	24oz (1½lb)
1kg	32oz (2lb)

oven temperatures

These oven temperatures are only a guide. Always check the manufacturer's manual.

	°C (Celsius)	°F (Fahrenheit)	Gas Mark
Very slow	120	250	1
Slow	150	300	2
Moderately slow	160	325	3
Moderate	180 – 190	350 – 375	4
Moderately hot	200 – 210	400 – 425	5
Hot	220 – 230	450 – 475	6
Very hot	240 – 250	500 – 525	7

liquid measures

metric	imperial
30ml	1 fluid oz
60ml	2 fluid oz
100ml	3 fluid oz
125ml	4 fluid oz
150ml	5 fluid oz (¼ pint/1 gill)
190ml	6 fluid oz
250ml	8 fluid oz
300ml	10 fluid oz (½ pint)
500ml	16 fluid oz
600ml	20 fluid oz (1 pint)
1000ml (1 litre)	1¾ pints

helpful measures

metric	imperial
3mm	⅛in
6mm	¼in
1cm	½in
2cm	¾in
2.5cm	1in
5cm	2in
6cm	2½in
8cm	3in
10cm	4in
13cm	5in
15cm	6in
18cm	7in
20cm	8in
23cm	9in
25cm	10in
28cm	11in
30cm	12in (1ft)

measuring equipment

The difference between one country's measuring cups and another's is, at most, within a 2 or 3 teaspoon variance. (For the record, one Australian metric measuring cup holds approximately 250ml.) The most accurate way of measuring dry ingredients is to weigh them. When measuring liquids, use a clear glass or plastic jug with metric markings. (For the record, one Australian metric tablespoon holds 20ml; one Australian metric teaspoon holds 5ml.)

Note: NZ, Canada, US and UK use 15ml tablespoons. All cup and spoon measurements are level.

We use large eggs with an average weight of 60g.

how to measure

When using graduated metric measuring cups, shake dry ingredients loosely into the appropriate cup. Do not tap the cup on a bench or tightly pack the ingredients unless directed to do so. Level top of measuring cups and measuring spoons with a knife. When measuring liquids, place a clear glass or plastic jug with metric markings on a flat surface to check accuracy at eye level.

Looking after **your interest...**

Keep your ACP cookbooks clean, tidy and within easy reach with slipcovers designed to hold up to 12 books. Plus you can follow our recipes perfectly with a set of accurate measuring cups and spoons, as used by *The Australian Women's Weekly* Test Kitchen.

To order

Mail or fax Photocopy and complete the coupon below and post to: ACP Books Reader Offer, ACP Publishing, GPO Box 4967, Sydney NSW 2001, or fax to (02) 9267 4967.

Phone Have your credit card details ready, then phone 136 116 (Mon-Fri, 8.00am-6.00pm; Sat, 8.00am-6.00pm).

Price

Book Holder

Australia: $13.10 (incl. GST).
Elsewhere: $A21.95.

Metric Measuring Set

Australia: $6.50 (incl. GST).
New Zealand: $A8.00.
Elsewhere: $A9.95.

Prices include postage and handling. This offer is available in all countries.

Payment

Australian residents

We accept the credit cards listed on the coupon, money orders and cheques.

Overseas residents

We accept the credit cards listed on the coupon, drafts in $A drawn on an Australian bank, and also UK, NZ and US cheques in the currency of the country of issue. Credit card charges are at the exchange rate current at the time of payment.

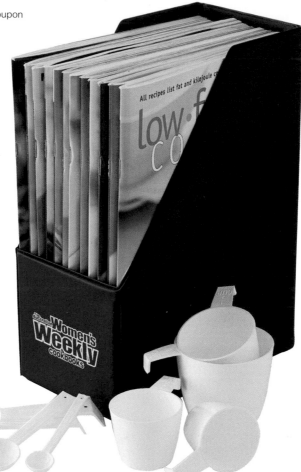

Photocopy and complete coupon below

Test Kitchen Staff
Food director *Pamela Clark*
Food editor *Karen Hammial*
Assistant food editor *Amira Ibram*
Test Kitchen manager *Kimberley Coverd*
Senior home economist *Cathie Lonnie*
Home economists *Sammie Coryton, Kelly Cruickshanks, Danielle Dive, Christina Martignago, Jessica Sly, Kirrily Smith, Kate Tait, Alison Webb*
Editorial coordinator *Rebecca Steyns*
Nutritional information *Laila Ibram*

ACP Books Staff
Editorial director *Susan Tomnay*
Creative director *Hieu Chi Nguyen*
Senior editors *Julie Collard; Wendy Bryan*
Designer *Mary Keep*
Studio manager *Caryl Wiggins*
Editorial/sales coordinator *Caroline Lowry*
Editorial assistant *Karen Lai*
Publishing manager (sales) *Brian Cearne*
Publishing manager (rights & new project*
 Jane Hazell
Brand manager *Donna Gianniotis*
Pre-press *Harry Palmer*
Production manager *Carol Currie*
Business manager *Seymour Cohen*
Assistant business analyst *Martin Howes*
Chief executive officer *John Alexander*
Group publisher *Pat Ingram*
Publisher *Sue Wannan*

Produced by ACP Books, Sydney.

Printed by Dai Nippon Printing in Korea.

Published by ACP Publishing Pty Limited
54 Park St, Sydney; GPO Box 4088,
Sydney, NSW 2001.
Ph: (02) 9282 8618 Fax: (02) 9267 9438.
acpbooks@acp.com.au
www.acpbooks.com.au
To order books, phone 136 116.
Send recipe enquiries to:
recipeenquiries@acp.com.au
AUSTRALIA: Distributed by Network Serv
GPO Box 4088, Sydney, NSW 2001.
Ph: (02) 9282 8777 Fax: (02) 9264 3278.
UNITED KINGDOM: Distributed by Austra
Consolidated Press (UK), Moulton Park
Business Centre, Red House Rd,
Moulton Park, Northampton, NN3 6AQ.
Ph: (01604) 497 531 Fax: (01604) 497 53
acpukltd@aol.com
CANADA: Distributed by Whitecap Books
351 Lynn Ave, North Vancouver, BC, V7J 2
Ph: (604) 980 9852 Fax: (604) 980 8197
customerservice@whitecap.ca
www.whitecap.ca
NEW ZEALAND: Distributed by Netlink
Distribution Company, ACP Media Centre
Cnr Fanshawe and Beaumont Streets,
Westhaven, Auckland.
PO Box 47906, Ponsonby, Auckland, NZ.
Ph: (9) 366 9966 ask@ndcnz.co.nz

Clark, Pamela.
The Australian Women's Weekly
Lean Food.

Includes index.
ISBN 1 86396 337 5